STUDIES IN HISTORY, ECONOMICS AND PUBLIC LAW

Edited by the
FACULTY OF POLITICAL SCIENCE
OF COLUMBIA UNIVERSITY

NUMBER 474

DISCUSSION OF HOLIDAYS IN THE LATER MIDDLE AGES

BY

EDITH COOPERRIDER RODGERS

DISCUSSION OF HOLIDAYS
IN THE
LATER MIDDLE AGES

BY

EDITH COOPERRIDER RODGERS

AMS PRESS, INC.
NEW YORK
1967

PREFACE

THIS monograph is an outgrowth of a suggestion by Professor Lynn Thorndike to investigate further such writings critical of holidays as the treatise *De novis celebritatibus non instituendis* of Nicolas de Clémanges. From this beginning the investigation has broadened to its present scope. A large amount of material pertaining to the study was found to be available, through early or modern editions, in New York and other eastern cities. Since many of the works are ecclesiastical, the Library of Union Theological Seminary has served as a nucleus. Its excellent collection of incunabula has been supplemented by fifteenth-century volumes from the Morgan Library, and the rare-book rooms of Columbia and Harvard Universities, the New York Public Library, the Library of Congress, the Henry Charles Lea Library of the University of Pennsylvania, and the Library of the College of Physicians in Philadelphia. The author welcomes the opportunity to express again her appreciation of the facilities which these libraries have placed at her disposal. Special acknowledgment to the staff of the Columbia Library and that of Union Theological Seminary is made for their unfailing kindness throughout the course of this inquiry.

To the Metropolitan Museum of Art the writer is grateful for various series of lectures, which have substantially increased her understanding of the iconography of the Middle Ages.

Warm thanks are due to Professor Austin Evans, who has read these chapters in an unfinished state, and given valued advice and assistance. Professor Eugene Byrne and Dr. William Rockwell have likewise offered helpful suggestions in regard to the text. To Professor Lynn Thorndike the author owes much of her interest in intellectual history. His scholarly aid and friendly counsel over a period of years have brought a debt of gratitude which she cannot hope to discharge.

E. C. R.

NEW YORK
MAY, 1940.

CONTENTS

CHAPTER I

INTRODUCTION

THIS study of holidays in the Middle Ages is concerned chiefly with the attitudes of medieval people toward them. From such an angle, the place which men allotted to holidays in their scheme of life, and the ways in which they employed the leisure that holidays afforded, become considerations of importance. In the shaping of contemporary views, it is not surprising that the Church exercised the dominant influence, inasmuch as holy days were essentially an ecclesiastical matter. Between its traditional teaching and the practical application of its lessons, however, lay a difference, for the standard which it set was the mirror of perfection; the counsel which it offered seemed often a plan ill-devised to meet the needs of folk upon whom secular affairs pressed with increasing weight. What stand the Church took in respect to holidays, what forces both within and without its circle attacked this position during the three hundred and twenty odd years between the opening of the thirteenth century and the Reformation, and what attempts were made to stem the onslaught of criticism directed against such holidays form the subject of this inquiry.

As a convenient point of departure, the year 1200 A.D. has been chosen arbitrarily. By that date pagan rites which the Church wished to preserve, or was unable to eradicate, had become imbued with new significance; pagan deities had been supplanted by Christian saints; and the policy of the Church respecting holy days had received canonical definition. Of the importance of holidays, some idea may be gained from a casual glance at the official ecclesiastical calendar of the period as set forth in Gratian's *Decretum*.[1] In the section entitled *De consecratione* are listed for observance all Sundays and thirty-six feast days (if one reckons the days following Pentecost as two,

---

1 Pars III, dist. iii, c. 1; see *Corpus iuris canonici*, edited by E. A. von Friedberg (Leipzig, 1879-1881), I, 1353.

and those of the Apostles as nine, for according to western usage the feasts of Peter and Paul, of Simon and Jude, and of Philip and James the Less, were given joint celebration). By the time Gregory IX issued his *Decretals* the situation in regard to the major holidays of the Church showed no decided change, for the paragraph *Conquestus est nobis,* which applies to the observance of holidays on which no legal business was to be transacted, lists forty feast days in addition to the Sundays.[2] The difference between this tabulation and that of the *Decretum* lies in its omission of the three Rogation Days, and its inclusion of an additional feast of the Virgin and of the week preceding Easter.

At the close of both canons stands an injunction to parishioners to celebrate any other feasts which met with the approval of their bishops. In the latitude of this provision lay the source of much future difficulty. Designed to afford opportunity for the observance of days of local significance,[3] it tended to lengthen the calendar unduly, and often resulted in the establishment of holidays in honor of persons whose attainments scarcely justified the bestowal of such dignity.[4] How frequently

2 Lib. II, tit. ix, c. 5 (*Corp. iur. canon.,* II, 272-73). A more generous interpretation of this canon, and that of Gratian, makes the number of holy days even larger. See the article "Feasts" in the *Catholic Encyclopedia.*

3 Maximus of Turin, Homily 81, *Patrologiae cursus completus. Series latina.* Edited by J. P. Migne (Paris, 1844-64), LVII, 427. See also R. T. Hampson, *Medii aevi kalendarium* (London, 1841), pp. 36-37. By the twelfth century interest in local saints had begun to manifest itself in monumental art. (J. Evans, *Life in Mediaeval France* [London, 1925], pp. 170-71.) For a discussion of the appearance of national saints, see W. H. Hutton, *The Influence of Christianity upon National Character, Illustrated by the Lives and Legends of the English Saints* (London, 1903).

4 Lanfranc's concern about the purely local character of many early English saints led him to consult Anselm regarding their right to sanctity. See Eadmer, *De vita et conversatione Anselmi Archiepiscopi Cantuariensis,* edited by M. Rule (London, 1884), pp. 350-53. For the "popular canonization" of Simon de Montfort and that of his son, whose claim to sanctity rested, in the case of the elder, on his part in the Albigensian Crusade, and, in the case of the younger, on his championing of the liberal cause against Henry III, see G. G. Coulton, *Five Centuries of Religion* (Cambridge, 1923-36),

circumstances of this sort occurred, may be surmised from the repeated emphasis of conciliar decrees, provincial ordinances, and comments of canonists upon the fact that the aforesaid selective power should apply only to saints recognized by the Apostolic See.[5] In many instances, however, popular acclaim preceded official sanction.[6]

Although medieval calendars obviously can receive but scant consideration here, it is worth while to note in passing that exercise of the diocesan right of option gave rise to calendar variations which often reflected regional interests. Sometimes patrons of the city or country, former bishops or martyrs of a district, or saints whose relics a community might possess were represented in the local calendar. It is therefore not surprising to find Edward the Confessor, Edmund King and Martyr, George, Dunstan, Alban, Etheldreda, and Thomas à Becket among the saints whose feast days were observed in the province of Canterbury.[7] For the same reasons Wenceslas, Procopius, and Ludmilla were revered at Prague;[8] Florianus, Proculus, and

III, 110; and Hutton, *op. cit.*, pp. 269 ff. For the veneration accorded Henry VI and Archbishop Scrope by political adherents, see *Fabric Rolls of York Minster,* edited by J. Raine (Durham, etc., 1859), pp. 82, 208 ff; and 193-96.

5 See Johannes Andreae, *Liber sextus decretalium . . . cum apparatu Johannis Andree* (Nuremberg, 1482), under " De reliquiis et veneratione sanctorum"; G. Durandus, *Speculum* (Lyons, 1547), II, fol. 6or, col. 1; Astesanus de Asta, *Summa de casibus conscientiae* (Eichstadt, 1480), lib. I, tit. xxiii, c. 1.

6 The veneration accorded Thomas à Becket and Osmund of Salisbury serve as examples. Owing to the circumstances of his death, the former was regarded as a saint almost immediately, although his veneration did not receive papal approval until 1173. The canonization of the latter was, however, a much longer process. Application was first made by the bishop of Salisbury in 1228. (*Concilia Magnae Britanniae et Hiberniae,* edited by D. Wilkins, [London, 1737], I, 561). Only after repeated requests (1387, 1406, 1417, 1424, 1441, 1452) was the bull of canonization finally issued by Calixtus III, in 1456.

7 *Sacrorum conciliorum nova et amplissima collectio,* edited by J. D. Mansi and others (Florence and Venice, 1759-98), XXII, 1153, c. viii.

8 *Ibid.,* XXVI, 398, c. xlvi.

Petronius at Bologna;[9] Miniatus and Zenobius at Florence;[10] and Sernin and Exuperius at Toulouse.[11] Sometimes, to be sure, choice was determined largely by the reputed power of a saint to ward off special forms of disaster. For instance, as guardian against sudden death, St. Christopher was often listed in the calendar of a community, and the inclusion of St. Nicholas was considered insurance against perils of the sea. In numerous calendars appeared the names of early Christian figures who seem to have had little connection with the districts which kept their festivals. Often these were persons who had never been formally canonized, but to whom a place in the hierarchy of saints had been assigned by custom. Since many of this goodly band were martyrs and confessors who, through association with some chapter of Roman history, had found representation in the calendar of Rome itself, Bishop Dowden has suggested that the introduction of their names into the roster of saints in other localities tends to show the widely disseminated influence of the calendar of the Eternal City.[12]

The saints of whom mention has been made had already received recognition by the year 1200. In the course of the following three and a quarter centuries, the canonization of well known persons who had taken an active part in the religious, intellectual, or political movements of their time substantially increased the number of holy days. Among these were Anthony of Padua, Francis of Assisi, Dominic, Thomas Aquinas, Elizabeth of Hungary, Louis IX of France, Bernardino of Siena,

9 *Statuti delle università ... dello studio bolognese*, edited by C. Malagola (Bologna, 1888), pp. 101-103.

10 *Statuti della Repubblica Fiorentina*, edited by R. Caggese (Florence, 1910-21), II, 95-96.

11 Calendar of the University of Toulouse; see M. Fournier, *Les statuts et privilèges des universités françaises depuis leur fondation jusqu'en 1789* (Paris, 1890-94), I, 467-68.

12 J. Dowden, *The Church Year and Kalendar* (Cambridge, 1910), pp. 24-25. In similar fashion, the appearance of such names as Brice, Remigius, Hilary of Poitiers, and Lambert of Liège in English calendars may be attributed to Norman-French influence.

Antonino of Florence, Bonaventura, Catherine of Siena, Hugh
of Lincoln, Bridget of Sweden, and Edmund of Abingdon, to
enumerate only a few. For one reason or another, less prominent
people like Peter Martyr of Milan, Louis of Toulouse, Nicholas
of Tolentino, Hedwiga of Silesia, Thomas Cantelupe, and
Peter de Murrone, better known as Celestine V, were enrolled
among the saints. Extension of the cult of the Virgin added
the feasts of St. Joseph, of the Visitation, and of the Presentation in the Temple. Other festivals such as the Feast of Corpus
Christi, which had been locally celebrated for some time, were
given official sanction and prescribed for the Church as a
whole.[13]

Information about canonizations and the consequent multiplication of feast days may be ascertained in fair degree. Less
easily determined, however, are questions pertaining to the actual number of holidays celebrated by individual communities,
and the strictness with which localities enforced their observance. Modern writers, whose attention appears to be centered
upon the economic aspects of the problem, hold by no means
unanimous views regarding the matter. Some believe that the
medieval laborer lost much time through compulsory idleness on
holy days, and could therefore seldom count upon a full week's
wage;[14] another maintains that he worked fairly continuously,
and really enjoyed few holidays;[15] and still others, adopting a
middle position, grant the inconvenience of holy days, but feel
that the respite from toil which was thus afforded a heavily-

13 For detailed information regarding these saints and their days, see
Acta sanctorum Bollandiana, January-November 10 (Paris, etc., 1863 ff) ; F.
G. Holweck, *A Biographical Dictionary of the Saints* (St. Louis, etc., 1924) ;
S. Baring-Gould, *Lives of the Saints* (Edinburgh, 1914).

14 W. Denton, *England in the Fifteenth Century* (London, 1888), pp. 219,
222. See also F. W. Tickner's *Social and Industrial History of England*
(New York, 1923), p. 62. *Cf.* W. Cunningham, *Growth of English Industry
and Commerce* (Cambridge, 1910-12), I, 390-91 and 449.

15 J. E. T. Rogers, *A History of Agriculture and Prices in England,
1259-1793* (Oxford, 1866-1902), I, 256; also his *Six Centuries of Work and
Wages* (New York, 1884), p. 181.

burdened people tended to compensate for this disadvantage.[16] Difference in the interpretation of documents,[17] and difficulties inherent in an investigation of the holiday problem suggest two plausible explanations for the divergence of these opinions.

For a study of holy days, contemporary materials are widely scattered geographically, and unevenly distributed in point of time. With few exceptions, the information available occurs in fragmentary form and must be pieced together in painstaking fashion. The final result is therefore not unlike a mosaic. Many and varied, however, are the sources from which facts about holidays may be gleaned. They include, for example, theological treatises, sermons, decrees of ecclesiastical synods and councils, episcopal visitations, university statutes, records of towns and gilds, expense accounts, fabric and manor rolls, legal documents, chronicles, and literature in the vernacular. Inasmuch as choice of material often predetermines a writer's conclusions, some evaluation of types of source may not be amiss.

By way of approach, calendars, of which mention has already been made, offer the most obvious information concerning holy days. In cases where these consist merely of a chronological arrangement of saints' days observed in particular localities, their usefulness for our purpose is somewhat limited.[18] If, however, annotations have been added, or instructions about the nature of the observance are given, they usually prove of

16 L. F. Salzmann, *English Industries of the Middle Ages* (Boston, etc., 1913), p. 212. See also H. S. Bennett, *Life on the English Manor* (Cambridge, 1937), p. 115.

17 In reckoning the agricultural work of the year, Walter of Henley, in his *Husbandry* (p. 9), allows eight weeks for holy days and other hindrances. Rogers assumes that Sundays fall within this exemption (*Six Centuries of Work and Wages*, p. 181). Since agricultural work was forbidden on Sundays, Maitland excludes these days as a matter of course (*Domesday Book and Beyond* [Cambridge, 1921], p. 398). The difference in the number of holy days is considerable.

18 Most calendars are of this sort. See Mansi, XXII, 1136, c. iv; XXIII, 870, c. xxi; XXVI, 398, c. xlvi; and Wilkins, *Concilia*, II, 145, c. xxiii; III, 252.

greater interest. In university calendars inclusions of this sort are not infrequent. There we read that a holy day which has been neglected for some time is again to be celebrated;[19] that cognizance of a recent canonization has been taken in the addition of the saint's feast to the calendar;[20] that festivals of major importance are to be honored by the suspension of regular lectures;[21] that some holidays, recognized by one faculty, need not be observed by another;[22] that St. Luke's Day shall mark the beginning of the academic term, even in years in which this feast chances to fall upon a Sunday.[23] In ecclesiastical calendars notations are employed more sparingly, and usually serve merely to indicate the importance of holidays by classifying them as simple or double feasts.[24] Sometimes meagre information of this kind is supplemented by remarks about the character of the procession,[25] the part played by the choir,[26] or the number of lessons to be used on these occasions.[27] Despite its technical nature, such comment suggests, in indirect fashion, the splendor of the service on the principal festivals of the Church,

19 *Auctarium chartularii universitatis Parisiensis,* edited by H. Denifle, A. Chatelain, C. Samaran, and others (Paris, 1894-1938), III, 118, 147-48. Owing to lack of funds and the building of the schools, the Feast of St. Nicholas had been neglected for two years by the English-German nation.

20 A fifteenth-century revision of the statutes of the University of Bologna adds the name of Bernardino of Siena to the calendar. *Statuti,* p. 194. (Bernardino was canonized in 1450; his feast day is May 20). The name of Louis of Toulouse (canonized in 1317 by John XXII) appears in the calendar included in the statutes of the years 1317-1347. *Statuti,* p. 41, n. 1.

21 *Ancient Kalendar of the University of Oxford from Documents of the Fourteenth to the Seventeenth Century,* edited by C. Wordsworth (Oxford, 1904), pp. xiv-xxv.

22 (Univ. of Paris), *Chart. univ. Paris.,* II, pt. 1, 709-16, *passim.*

23 (Univ. of Avignon), Fournier, *op. cit.,* II, 311.

24 *The Sarum Missal in English,* translated by F. E. Warren (London, 1911), pp. 1-12.

25 *Missale ad usum insignis ecclesiae Eboracensis,* edited by W. G. Henderson (Durham, 1874), vol. I, *passim.*

26 *Ibid.,* vol. II, *passim.*

27 *Sarum Missal,* pp. 1-12.

when rich music, brilliant sacerdotal vestments, and an elaborate ritual were the order of the day.

In the decrees of ecclesiastical councils, the paragraphs pertaining to holy days often bear semblance to calendars, in that they enumerate systematically, and frequently without comment, the feast days meriting celebration. From material in which we may reasonably expect to find expression of the policy of the Church toward holidays, such stereotyped reference to the subject is distinctly disappointing. For our purpose, provincial or diocesan legislation sometimes proves more satisfactory than do ecumenical decrees, for the former occasionally mentions the circumstances which have evoked the holiday statute, or indicates the result which it is expected to accomplish.[28] Although in most cases conformity to established rule and custom appears to have been the end in view, need for a revision of the attitude of the Church in regard to the whole question made itself felt from time to time, especially in the programs of reform which were formulated, often at papal request, before the convening of the general councils of the fourteenth and fifteenth centuries. Had the criticism of holiday abuses offered by such churchmen as Guillaume le Maire of Angers[29] and the younger William Durand of Mende[30] to the council of Vienne in 1311, and by Pierre d'Ailly[31] and Francesco Zabarella of Florence[32] at the time of the Council of Constance, not been set aside by considerations of a more immediate nature,

28 Council of Exeter; see Mansi, XXIV, 812, c. xxiii.

29 *Livre de Guillaume le Maire,* edited by M. C. Port (Paris, n. d.) ; also in *Collection de documents inédits sur l'histoire de France. Mélanges historiques,* XI, pt. 2, pp. 187-569.

30 "Tractatus de modo generalis concilii celebrandi", see *Tractatus illustrium in utraque tum pontificii, tum caesarei iuris facultate iurisconsultorum,* XIII (Lyons, 1584), pt. I, fols. 154 r-182 v.

31 "Tractatus de reformatione, seu canones reformandi ecclesiam", see H. von der Hardt, *Magnum oecumenicum Constantiense concilium de universali ecclesiae reformatione . . .* I, 409-433; or J. Gerson, *Opera omnia,* II, 903-916.

32 "Capita agendorum in concilio generali Constantiensi de reformatione ecclesiae", see H. von der Hardt, *op. cit.,* I, 490-536.

we should probably find the acts of the aforesaid assemblies more useful for our study.

From the frequency with which medieval theologians and jurists referred to that portion of canon law which pertains to holy days,[33] we might expect to find the subject presented in greater detail. The paragraphs are, however, few, and the number of points considered is small. In addition to enumerating the feasts marked for celebration, the canons deal briefly with the observance of Sunday, the length of holy days, and the conditions under which servile labor might legitimately be performed at such times. Inasmuch as these matters are treated in general terms, interpretation of the policy of the Church fell to the lot of canonists, who, in the performance of this task, leaned heavily upon the corresponding section of the *Corpus iuris civilis*,[34] as does canon law itself. Some authorities, like Alexander of Hales (d. 1245), whose chief interest lay in theology rather than in law, presented their views under a discussion of the third commandment;[35] others, like Raymond of Pennafort (d. 1275)[36] and Henry of Susa (Hostiensis, d. 1271),[37] followed in their *Summae* the conventional method of using the titles of canon law for paragraph headings. Since a similar practice prevailed among jurists in regard to the civil law, we find in the works of such eminent lawyers as Oldrado da Ponte (d. 1335),[38] Bartolo da Sassoferrato (1314-1357),[39]

33 See J. B. Sägmüller, *Lehrbuch des katholischen Kirchenrechts* (3rd edition, Freiburg, 1914), II, 272.

34 The section "De feriis" in the *Digest* is found in Vol. I, Bk. II, tit. xii. An English translation is available in C. H. Munro's work, *The Digest of Justinian* (Cambridge, 1904-09), I, pp. 98-101.

35 *Summa theologiae* (Nuremberg, 1481-82), pars III, quaestio xxxii, "De tercio mandato decalogi."

36 *Summa* (Verona, 1744). Titulus XII is entitled "De feriis, et festis, et diebus jejuniorum."

37 *Summa aurea* (Venice, 1586).

38 *Consilia, seu responsa, et quaestiones aureae, in quibus ea quae ad quotidianum usum in forensibus negotiis, et controversiis spectant, subtilissime et exactissime perstringuntur* (Venice, 1571).

39 *Omnia quae extant opera,* see Vol. VII, "Commentaria" (Venice, 1590).

and Baldo degli Ubaldi (1327?-1400),[40] under the title *De feriis,* comments on occasional cases which have to do with holidays. Since these suits often center about such questions as the validity of donations made on holy days,[41] or the legality of exacting confessions[42] or of apprehending criminals on such occasions,[43] feast days and their observance obviously constituted a problem of more than religious significance.

Although few treatises on holy days appeared during the Middle Ages, discussion of some aspect of the subject is to be found in a variety of works. The ritualist William Durand (d. 1237-1296), for example, devoted a chapter of his *Rationale divinorum officiorum* to the liturgical usages employed on feasts and festivals;[44] Antonino of Florence considered the neglect of feast days in his *Summa theologica,* or compendium of moral theology;[45] and Bernardino of Siena (1380-1444) treated the observance of Sunday and the celebration of feast days in a lengthy Latin sermon intended for readers rather than hearers.[46] Authors, like Alvaro Pelayo (d. ca. 1352),[47] who wrote critical estimates of the Church, and others, like Wyclif (1324 ?-1384),[48] who advocated its reformation, also touched upon the matter of holy days. So, too, did churchmen who, like John Mirk (fl. 1403), wrote didactic works for the guidance of the parish priest.[49] To all of these men holidays constituted merely

40 *Consilia* (Venice, 1608-09).

41 Oldradus, *Consilia,* fol. 116 r and v (consil. 253).

42 Bartolus, *Opera,* VII, 99v, col. 1.

43 Baldus, *Consilia,* V, 42v (consil. 166).

44 Lib. VII: "De sanctorum festivitatibus", fols. 424-468.

45 Pars II, tit. ix, c. vii, cols. 975-87, is devoted to "De negligentia circa observationem festorum."

46 *Opera omnia,* edited by J. de la Haye (Venice, 1745), II, 51-63. This sermon is entitled "De observantia Sabbati et celebratione festorum."

47 *De planctu ecclesiae* (Ulm, 1474).

48 *Select English Works,* edited by T. Arnold (Oxford, 1869), *Wyclif's English Works Hitherto Unprinted,* edited by F. D. Matthew (London, 1880).

49 *Instructions for Parish Priests,* edited by E. Peacock (London, 1868), and Antoninus of Florence, *Confessionale* (Strassburg, 1490).

one approach to a larger problem, and consequently the attention which they gave to the matter was comparatively slight. A
few theologians, however, thought the question of holy days
worthy of distinct treatment. Aside from indicating an interest in the subject, these treatises usually add little to our
knowledge, for they either partake of the formal scholastic
character of the earlier *Summae confessorum* or turn out to be
compilations of information about the lives of saints, such as
we find in many martyrologies. Under the first heading fall
tractates like that of Henry of Gorichem (d. 1460) on the celebration of feasts,[50] and in the second category come a number
of works which appear in the manuscript catalogues of Euro-
pean libraries under a variety of titles pertaining to the observance of Sundays and feast days.[51]

Proposals to add new holidays to the calendar provoked
works of greater importance. Among these, the treatise of
Nicolas de Clémanges (1360-1437?) concerning the non-
establishment of new solemnities is the most useful and best
known.[52] Written between 1408 and 1412, after his retirement
from Avignon, where he had acted as secretary to Benedict
XIII until the time of the anti-pope's quarrel with Charles VI,
this treatise, in its use of invective, reflects the bitterness of the
conflict which raged during the turbulent years of the Great
Schism. Despite this bias and the rhetorical lengths to which a
Ciceronian style leads him, it is obvious that Clémanges understood the problems which the multiplication of holy days raised,
and that he had given them sufficient thought to suggest solu-
tions to them. In all probability, the work is largely an expression of contemporary opinion. This fact, however, in no way
weakens the force of the argument, which must have impressed
his own as well as subsequent generations. The clarity with

---

50 *Tractatus de celebratione festorum* (Esslingen, 1474?).

51 *Promptuarium discipuli de festis sanctorum intimandis et dominicis
diebus* (1465), CLM 1224, 1-34, for example, is a martyrology.

52 "De novis celebritatibus non instituendis", *Opera omnia,* edited by J.
M. Lydius (Leyden, 1613), I, 143-60.

which Clémanges defined the situation doubtless accounts in part for the non-appearance of comparable treatises on the subject.

A similar, but less substantial, thesis is that of the Zurich precentor Felix Hemmerlin (d. ca. 1460) concerning the institution of new offices.[53] Presentation of a sum of money to be used by the canons of Zurich in celebrating the Feast of St. Francis with ceremony equal to that employed on St. John's Day furnished the occasion for this work, which is a direct protest against the bestowal of additional honor upon St. Francis.[54] Incidentally, however, the treatise voices objection to the accumulation of holidays in general. Although Hemmerlin's criticism is based largely upon disapproval of a current tendency to raise the status of established feast days, Balthasar Reber is probably correct in surmising that it was dislike of the Franciscans which prompted the author to condemn the aforesaid practice at this particular time.[55] Since Hemmerlin had been identified with the reform party at the Council of Basel, and obviously knew what discussion the matter of holy days had elicited there and at the Council of Constance, it is disappointing to find the tenor of his argument so inconsequential.

In medieval sermons there is also less expression of critical opinion concerning holidays and their observance than might be supposed from the fact that the pulpit has always served as an instrument for the correction of ills. It is not surprising that such a work as Mirk's *Festial*,[56] designed to teach people about important feasts of the liturgical year, should be unsuited to

53 "Tractatus de novorum officiorum divinorum institutione", *Variae oblectationis opuscula et tractatus* (Strassburg, 1498), fols. 43r-52r.

54 In Hemmerlin's estimation, there was a difference between the feast day of a mere confessor like St. Francis and that of a "doctor", a pope, or a great figure like John the Baptist. Since Christ himself had said that his Father's house included many mansions, he saw no reason why all saints should be accorded equal honor.

55 B. Reber, *Felix Hemmerlin von Zürich* (Zurich, 1846), p. 311.

56 A collection of homilies, edited by T. Erbe (London, 1905).

our needs, since homilies are essentially didactic in character. Equally unsatisfactory are most sermons entitled *De tempore et de sanctis,* in that they usually prove to be discourses on abstract virtues or summaries of the lives of saints, with reflections on the lessons to be drawn from such noteworthy examples of Christian piety.[57] Among popular preachers of the Mendicant Orders abstractions found little favor. Interest in the contemporary scene often led these men to direct the attention of their congregations to social faults and questions of the day. For this reason, their sermons include occasional criticism of holy days or of holiday behavior. In Berthold von Regensburg's condemnation of dancing, for example, we not only encounter the conventional attitude of the Church toward a popular form of holiday amusement, but also see the indignant surprise of a thirteenth-century audience at the Franciscan's insistence that this form of recreation be abandoned on feast days.[58] From Jacques de Vitry's good-humored reminder that the difficulty of keeping track of church holidays is greatly obviated by regular church attendance, we learn that holy days were numerous, ill-kept, and frequently a source of contention between clergy and laity.[59] Bernardino of Siena's denunciation of the Saturday half-holiday shows us the prejudice of some medieval theologians against Sabbatarian practices which savored, they said, of Jewish superstitions.[60] Absorption in secular affairs on feast days, neglect of holiday obligations, and the multiplication of misdemeanors and crimes at times of high festival are also mentioned in the discourses of other divines. When these references occur incidentally, they have little of the polemic about them, and so often prove of greater value than

57 See Albertus Magnus, "Sermons", *Opera omnia* (Paris, 1890-99), XIII, 407-663, for example.

58 Berthold von Regensburg, *Vollständige Ausgabe seiner Predigten,* edited by F. Pfeiffer and J. Strobl (Vienna, 1862-1880), I, 268-269.

59 *The Exempla or Illustrative Stories from the Sermones Vulgares of Jacques de Vitry,* edited by T. F. Crane (London, 1890), p. 77.

60 *Opera omnia,* II, 54, col. 1. See also the gloss of Hostiensis on the *Decret. Greg. IX,* lib. II, tit. ix, c. 3, in his *Summa aurea,* col. 516.

would a diatribe upon the subject. To strengthen the force of argument, preachers sometimes selected, from the *exempla* at hand, stories which met their needs, or could be adapted to their purpose. The sparing use of this type of illustration may be explained by the fact that many medieval tales pertaining to holy days have to do with the misfortunes and disasters visited upon those who failed to heed ecclesiastical admonitions regarding holiday observance. Narratives concerned, for example, with injury to a hand through picking peas on a saint's day,[61] or with the dire consequences of felling a tree upon a Sunday,[62] partake of the miraculous, and occur most frequently in the early part of our period when theologians were debating the ceremonial and ethical nature of holiday observance. As a means of acquiring insight into the thought and feeling of medieval people toward holidays, sermons are exceedingly useful; they constitute, however, an unreliable source of information if depended upon exclusively, for the dramatic possibilities of his subject often tempted an eloquent preacher to stray beyond the bounds of accuracy.[63]

In an age in which confession was regarded as a universal obligation, it is not surprising that the prick of conscience prompted many to acknowledge infractions of the law on holy days. For the benefit of young or inexperienced priests per-

61 Despite the admonitions of the priest to celebrate with reverence the feast of St. Stephen, the patron saint of the parish, one man gathered peas. These clung to his hand so tightly that he finally betook himself to church, where, after prayers and devotions, he regained the use of it; not until the next day, however, was its full vigor restored. See Étienne de Bourbon, *Anecdotes historiques,* edited by A. Lecoy de la Marche (Paris, 1877), p. 273.

62 When the tree was struck, blood flowed from the wood. At a second stroke a voice cried, "Dimitte, dimitte". Additional blows led the voice to call down maledictions on him who sent the wood-cutter to fell the tree on so holy a day. Shortly thereafter, the young man who cut the tree died, and the Cistercian monk who had given the order disappeared, and was never seen in that region again. T. Wright, *Latin Stories* (London, 1842), pp. 76-77.

63 See J. F. Willard, " The Observances of Holidays and Vacations by the Lower Exchequer, 1327-1330 ", *University of Colorado Studies,* XXII (1935), 282.

plexed by difficulties presented to them in this way, and also for the edification of such of the laity as sought a guide to conduct, there appeared during the Middle Ages a series of manuals based on authoritative sources and the results of practical experience.[64] Under the heading of holidays (*feriae* or *de feriis*) these *Summae de casibus conscientiae* contain much useful material. In the earlier volumes, these sections often bear the imprint of the scholastic method, and are concerned primarily with such questions as these: Is the observance of Sunday to be termed moral or ceremonial?[65] Has Sunday replaced the Sabbath of the Old Testament?[66] Are holy days other than Sunday binding in character?[67] To be sure, consideration of what might or might not lawfully be done on such occasions was not neglected, but often greater interest was shown in the drawing of fine distinctions between the two classifications than in the matter itself. Since the first *Summae* served as models for later works of the kind, the aforesaid characteristics never entirely disappeared, although, in time, attention to practical problems assumed a larger place and dwarfed the scholastic tendencies previously noted. On moral questions, a few writers possessed of originality, or relatively unhampered by the bonds of authoritarianism, ventured to express opinions of their own, but in most instances authors relied upon the dicta given, under similar circumstances, by men like Thomas Aquinas (1225 ?-1274), Raymond of Pennafort, and Giovanni d'Andrea (d. 1348). In the *Summae,* as nowhere else, we find attempts of

64 A useful list of these works is given by Johannes Dietterle in his article "Die *Summae confessorum (sive de casibus conscientiae)* von ihren Anfängen an bis zu Silvester Prierias", *Zeitschrift für Kirchengeschichte,* XXIV (1903), 353-74, 520-548; XXV (1904), 248-72; XXVI (1905), 59-81, 350-62; XXVII (1906), 70-83, 166-188, 296-310, 431-442; XXVIII (1907), 401-431.

65 Johannes Friburgensis, *Summa confessorum* (Augsburg, 1476), lib. I, tit. xii, quaest. 5.

66 *Ibid.,* quaest. 6.

67 Monaldus, *Summa perutilis atque aurea* (Lyons, 1516?), fol. 76r; see also Bernardino of Siena, *Opera,* II, 54, col. 1.

priest and prelate to reconcile to the teachings of the Church current practices which they could not countenance, but were forced in some measure to accept. That literature of this sort constituted a potent factor in shaping contemporary views regarding holiday observances seems a safe assumption, inasmuch as its influence can be seen in the works of William Lyndwood,[68] Antonino of Florence,[69] and Thomas More.[70]

In continuity of record and variety of detail, university statutes, supplemented by muniments of a related sort, constitute a most satisfactory source of information concerning holidays. They cover practically our entire period; they represent organizations of different sizes and in many places; they deal with numerous aspects of university life. From their pages we learn how Sundays and feast days affected the student; what obligations fell upon him, what recreations and pursuits were permitted him, in what pranks and misdemeanors he was prone to indulge on such occasions. From contemporary student dialogues we may even hazard a guess as to what he thought and how he felt about holidays. That his sentiments did not always agree with those of the strict churchmen who framed the statutes is easily understandable.

Since the length of the working day and week has always been a matter of considerable importance, it is interesting to see what effect holy days had upon the economic life of the Middle Ages. Despite the impossibility of arriving at definite conclusions, we gain, from contemporary sources, an idea of the number of feast days observed, and learn, to some extent, whether such observance benefitted people, or imposed hardship upon them. For knowledge of holiday regulations in regard to the closing of shops, the plying of trades, the holding of

---

68 *Provinciale* (1679 ed.), pp. 101-102, Gloss a, and p. 103, Gloss o, refer to opinions of John of Freiburg.

69 Raymond of Pennafort is repeatedly quoted by Antonino.

70 In *The Apologye of Syr Thomas More, Knyght,* edited by A. I. Taft (London, 1930), p. 164, the *Summa rosella* of Baptista de Salis is given as authority.

markets, the transportation of merchandise, and the like, we are dependent in large measure, upon town documents and gild statutes. From such business records as fabric and manor rolls and expense accounts of various kinds, we are able to see, for limited periods, whether the prohibition against holiday labor was enforced. Excellent as is the material which these records often furnish, it must be acknowledged that the documents themselves frequently appear to be isolated examples of their kind. Even if we assume that they are typical of the period from which they come, there is little to recommend the practice of drawing general conclusions from sources widely separated in time and place. The fact that our investigation is concerned with the operation of ecclesiastical law, which, theoretically at least, was universal in its application, reduces to some extent the limitations of these materials.

Inasmuch as social and intellectual trends are often reflected in the literature of a period, medieval works of a popular nature, both in Latin and in the vernacular, offer a likely field for the expression of attitudes toward holy days. In exploring sources of this kind, it must not be forgotten that an author's purpose and his point of view frequently color his writings. From the *Canterbury Tales,* for instance, we must content ourselves with a few scattered references to saints and their days, since Chaucer is chiefly concerned with story-telling and the delineation of character. While he laughs at such human foibles as the hedonism of the Monk [71] or the cupidity of the Pardoner,[72] he is untroubled by the spirit of reform, and so shows no tendency to criticize institutions and customs. Although something of a moralist, the poet Gower (1325 ? -1408), like his contemporary Chaucer (1340-1400), makes little mention of holy days. To his interests as landed proprietor rather than as social critic is to be attributed his caustic comment upon the forms of amusement in which peasants indulge on holidays.[73]

71 *Prologue,* lines 165 ff.

72 *Ibid.,* lines 694 ff.

73 " Mirour de l'omme ", lines 8653 ff, Gower's *Works,* I, 101.

Since *Piers the Plowman* is essentially a didactic poem, we learn from Langland (1330 ? -1400 ?) what obligations devolved upon Christians on Sundays and feast days,[74] and what condemnation was visited upon those who failed to discharge these responsibilities.[75] Strong disapproval of the negligent keeping of holy days is also to be found in such works as *Handlyng Synne* [76] and its prototype *Le manuel des pechiez*.[77] Several tales by Boccaccio (1313-1375) deal with belief in the power of the saints,[78] but of people's feeling toward the festivals of the saints the *Decameron* tells us nothing. Since allegory is abstract, and largely constructive in design, works like the *Romance of the Rose* are equally useless for our purpose. In thirteenth-century satire, however, are found occasional examples of indifference to holiday observance, a respect in which peasants seem to have been the worst offenders, according to Gautier de Coincy [79] and the anonymous author of the [*Dit*] *des vingt-trois manières de vilains*.[80] With satirical humor, Erasmus, at a later day, calls attention to the evils of holiday practices,[81] and, in the same temper, the humanist Sebastian Brant (ca. 1457-1521)[82] and his clerical admirers Alexander

74 *The Vision of William Concerning Piers the Plowman,* edited by W. W. Skeat (Oxford, 1886), C VIII, 226; C X, 219 ff.

75 *Ibid.,* C X, 238-39; *cf.* A VIII, 20 ff. and B VII, 18 ff.

76 Robert Mannyng of Brunne, *Handlyng Synne,* edited by F. J. Furnivall (London, 1901).

77 By William of Wadington (ca. 1300) ; printed with Robert Mannyng's *Handlyng Synne.*

78 *Decameron,* II, 1, 2.

79 *Les miracles de la Sainte Vierge,* edited by M. l'Abbé Poquet (Paris, 1857), p. 625, lines 354-59.

80 [*Dit*] *des vingt-trois manières de vilains: pièce du XIIIᵉ siècle*; with a modern French translation by A. Jubinal (Paris, 1834).

81 In his " Colloquia familiaria " particularly; see *Opera,* edited by J. Clericus (Leyden, 1703-16), I, 627-890. For a translation of the " Colloquies ", see that by Nathan Bailey, 2 vols., London, 1878.

82 See his *Narrenschiff,* edited by Karl Simrock (Berlin, 1872). No. 95 (pp. 245-47) is entitled " Von Verführung am Feiertage."

Barclay (1475-1552)[83] and Geiler von Kaisersberg (1445-1510)[84] review the holiday follies of their time. In the form of dialogue, which proves an excellent medium for the presentation of conflicting points of view, the author of *Dives and Pauper,* in his consideration of the third commandment, gives a summary of early fifteenth-century opinion regarding holiday observance.[85] Surprisingly enough, literature devoted to the arraignment of society by classes contains only an occasional reference to holiday behavior, and the satire of the *fabliaux* is seldom, if ever, directed against holy days. Chronicles and local histories make only casual mention of feast days of special significance. Although the preceding references by no means exhaust the possibilities of literary allusion to our subject, the information to be derived from such sources is more meagre than might be supposed.

83 See his *Ship of Fools,* edited by T. H. Jamieson (Edinburgh, etc., 1874). "Of folys that kepe not the holy daye" is to be found in II, 174-78.

84 See his *Ausgewählte Schriften,* edited by Philip de Lorenzi (Trier, 1881).

85 *The Dialogue of Dives and Pauper: a compendyouse treatyse . . . fructuously treatynge upon the X Commandementes.* (Often attributed to Henry Parker. Wynken de Worde, 1496).

CHAPTER II

THE THEORY OF ORTHODOX HOLIDAY OBSERVANCE

In the year 1200, so chroniclers tell us,[1] Eustache, abbot of Flai, set out under papal commission for England, where, in accordance with the purport of a heaven-sent letter,[2] he preached against the non-observance of Sunday and saints' days. From the tenor of the chroniclers' accounts it appears, however, most unlikely that Eustache's mission was part of an organized movement under papal control, or that his zeal marked anything more significant than one of those periodical waves of Sabbatarianism which preceding generations had witnessed. Of a deep or a wide-spread interest in holy days during the early portion of the thirteenth century there is little evidence. At the Fourth Lateran Council the question of holiday observance seems not to have been mentioned,[3] although a war so recently waged against heretics might well have drawn attention to the fact that many dissident groups ignored Sundays, and that most of them had nothing but scorn for saints and their days.[4] Whether it was the menace of heresy,[5] or merely a

1 Roger of Hoveden, *Chronica*, edited by W. Stubbs (London, 1868-1871), IV, 167-168; Roger of Wendover, *Flores historiarum*, edited by H. G. Hewlett (London, 1886-1889), I, 296-297. For a recent estimate of his work, see J. L. Cate, " The English Mission of Eustace of Flay, 1200, 1201 ", *Études d'histoire dédiées à la mémoire de Henri Pirenne* (Brussels, 1937), pp. 67-89.

2 In slightly different form, this letter had appeared at intervals during the preceding centuries. An early English version is to be seen in John Audelay's poem on the observance of Sunday. *An English Miscellany, presented to Dr. Furnivall ...* (Oxford, 1901), pp. 397-407.

3 It has been suggested that market reform in England after 1218 was the result of papal influence. L. F. Salzman, *English Trade in the Middle Ages* (Oxford, 1931), p. 124.

4 Bernardus Guidonis, *Practica inquisitionis heretice pravitatis*, edited by C. Douais (Paris, 1886), pp. 246, 248; J. J. von Döllinger, *Beiträge zur Sektengeschichte des Mittelalters* (Munich, 1890), II, 9, 281; C. Schmidt,

tendency toward definition in a legalistic age, which led, in the *Decretals,* to elaboration of the policy of the Church toward holy days, cannot be determined. It is, however, fairly obvious that, from the second quarter of the thirteenth century to the Reformation, holidays and their observance were matters of general consideration.

Sunday was the most important of holy days, for it commemorated, in a mystic sense, the renewal of the world through Christ's resurrection. Inasmuch as its observance had not been ordained by divine law, this day, unlike the Sabbath of the Old Testament, was not regarded as inherently sacrosanct. Yet the very fact that it had been set aside by the Church and the custom of Christian people as a time for worship, contemplation, and rest [6] probably accounted for the feeling that there was to Sunday a permanence which holy days designated by papal decree did not enjoy.[7] Of unusual significance, and therefore worthy of exceptional honor, were days marking events in the life of Christ, the Virgin, and the Apostles. Easter and Pentecost merited special attention for this reason,[8] and such feasts as Christmas, the Epiphany, and Ascension Day were counted of greater significance than the ordinary Sunday.[9] Preeminence among the Apostles was accorded to Peter and Paul;[10]

Histoire et doctrine de la secte des Cathares ou Albigeois (Paris, 1849), II, 137-138.

5 Insistence upon church attendance and the observance of holy days is found in the decrees of many French councils of the period. *Sacrorum conciliorum . . . collectio,* ed. by Mansi, XXII, 786, c. iv, and 791, c. xvii (Avignon, 1209); *ibid.,* 834, c. iv, and 843, c. xviii (Paris, 1212); *ibid.,* 856, c. iv, and 857, c. vii (Const. of Pamiers, 1212); *ibid.,* 920, c. xix (Rouen, 1214); *ibid.,* 1136, c. iv (Toulouse, 1219); XXIII, 22, c. iii (Narbonne, 1227); *ibid.,* 200, c. xxv-xxvii (Toulouse, 1229); *ibid.,* 684, c. v (Meaux, 1245); *ibid.,* 701, c. xl (Béziers, 1246); *ibid.,* 732, c. ii (Nevers, 1246); *ibid.,* 750-51 (Le Mans, 1247); *ibid.,* 870, c. xxi (Cognac, 1255).

6 For a discussion of the Third Commandment, see Alexander of Hales Pars III, quaest, 32; Thomas Aquinas, Pars II, II, quaest. 122, art. 4.

7 *Handlyng Synne,* lines 807-812.

8 *Dives and Pauper,* " Third command.", chap. 10.

9 *Idem.*   10 Gratian, *Decretum, loc. cit.*

hence their festival, along with those of local and national saints, and the feast of the dedication of the church, were of primary interest. The greater number of holidays, however, consisted of saints' days of lesser importance, which depended, in large measure, for their status and the strictness of their observance upon the custom of the region.[11] To obviate difficulties arising from uncertainty as to which holy days appeared in the local calendar, various means were devised. In Norway, where parishes were, like that of Chaucer's Parson,[12] often wide and sparsely settled, church law stipulated that the approach of a holiday be indicated by the sending of a cross from door to door.[13] Most communities, however, adopted the less picturesque practice of reading at Sunday mass the list of holidays for the coming week.[14] Town officials, too, were not infrequently charged with the periodical publication of statutes dealing with holiday regulations,[15] and at universities the making of such announcements fell to the lot of the beadle.[16]

The Church was very insistent upon attendance at mass on Sundays and the important feasts of the year, when abstinence from servile work was enjoined.[17] With reverence and devotion, parishioners were expected to hear this office in its en-

11 Mansi, XXII, 1136, c. iv; W. Lyndwood, *Provinciale* (Glossed edition, Oxford, 1679), p. 101.

12 *Prologue,* lines 491 ff.

13 *The Earliest Norwegian Laws, being the Gulathing Law and the Frostathing Law,* translated by L. M. Larson (New York, 1935), pp. 47-48.

14 A. Lecoy de la Marche, *La chaire française au moyen âge* (Paris, 1886), p. 223; G. R. Owst, *Literature and Pulpit in Medieval England* (Cambridge, 1933), p. 123: "In alle the chirches of the worlde the prestes of hem, whiche are sette to the governaunce of the parishenes, aftur the redyng of the gospel and of the offertorie at masse, turne hem unto the peple and schewe openliche unto hem alle the solempnitees and festes which shall falle and be hadde in the weke folowynge."

15 *Corpus statutorum italicorum,* edited by Pietro Sella and others (Rome, 1912-33), VI, 296-297, c. 1; X, 46, c. lx.

16 *Munimenta academica,* edited by H. Anstey (London, 1868), II, 371; R. Kink, *Geschichte der Kaiserlichen Universität zu Wien* (Vienna, 1854), II, 86; Fournier, *Stat.... des univ. franç.,* II, 671; III, 79.

17 Mansi, XXIII, 874, c. xxxvi; *ibid.,* 1031, c. iv; Wilkins, III, 43.

tirety.[18] If they grew careless about attending the service from beginning to end, it became the duty of confessors to learn whether negligence, contempt, love of gain, or fondness for recreation was the occasion thereof.[19] Such a task might well have proved a burden to conscientious clergymen, for, from sermons and *exempla,* we are led to believe that promptness was not a common virtue.[20] Among those who arrived late and withdrew early, students seem to have been the worst offenders, for some universities found it necessary to impose fines for tardiness and untimely departure. The amount of the levy depended upon the status of the student and the point in the service at which he entered or left the chapel.[21] Church attendance on holy days was, of course, not always possible. Illness,[22] absence from the district, especially on military duty,[23] and dire necessity,[24] constituted legitimate excuses for non-appearance. Repeated absence without excuse made offenders liable to fine, and, in extreme cases, even to excommunication.[25]

Difference of opinion prevailed concerning the importance of the sermon on Sundays and feast days. It is not surprising that Bernardino of Siena, one of the Friars Minor, should

18 Bernardino of Siena reminds his congregation that public worship must not be considered a formality; it ought to be accompanied by prayers which rise from the heart. See *Opera*, II, 59, col. 2.

19 Antoninus of Florence, *Confessionale*, fol. 45v; see also Gerson, II, 560, 561.

20 Bernardino, III, 265, col. 1; *Dives and Pauper,* "First command.", chap. 51.

21 *Statutes of Brasenose College* (London, 1853), pp. 18-19; (Cart. of Montpellier), see Fournier, *Stat....des univ. franç.*, I, 303.

22 *Veterum scriptorum et monumentorum amplissima collectio*, edited by E. Martène and U. Durand (2nd ed., Paris, 1724-33), VII, 106; Angelus Carletus, fol. 128 v, § 42; *Piers the Plowman*, B V, 458 ff.

23 Mansi, XXII, 1135, c. ii; Wilkins, III, 11, c. vi; Angelus Carletus, fol. 128 v, § 42.

24 Mansi, XXII, 768, c. xi.

25 Mansi, XXII, 1135, c. ii, and XXIII, 200, c. xxv (for examples of fine); see also XXVI, 520, c. lxxxiv (for threats of excommunication). Bernardino of Siena felt that excuses were often given on insufficient grounds (*Opera*, II, 62, col. 1).

have emphasized this part of the service, for he saw therein opportunity for explanation of the Law and the teaching of Gospel.[26] The significance of the sermon, from a social point of view, was not to be lightly regarded in an age when education of the masses depended so largely upon oral instruction. Bernardino therefore insisted that the orthodoxy of the preacher be assured.[27] Danger from heresy William of Wykeham regarded as such a menace that, in establishing New College, he provided for only one sermon during the year. This fell on the Feast of the Annunciation.[28] On Sundays and other holy days, he stipulated that the College attend matins, mass, and first and second vespers, and march in procession about the cloisters in surplice and hood.[29] With so large a portion of the day allotted to religious exercises, Wykeham probably thought it extremely unlikely that the sermons offered at St. Mary's,[30] or elsewhere in Oxford, would present a sore temptation to students.

According to strict interpretation, holiday obligations to Holy Church were not to be lightly discharged by attendance at mass. Holy days of prime importance were to be spent in serious and profitable manner.[31] On Sundays especially, the parishioner was urged to bestir himself as zealously in God's service as he labored in his own behalf on other days of the week.[32] Examination of conscience,[33] the amendment of faults,[34]

---

26 *Opera,* III, 169, col. 1. In the same sermon, Bernardino says that, if people cannot hear both the mass and the sermon, they should choose the sermon, because, through preaching, they come from knowledge to faith. On Sunday and other days of obligation, they have, however, no choice in the matter, for then attendance at mass is enjoined.

27 Bernardino, III, 169, col. 2.

28 H. Rashdall and R. S. Rait, *New College* (London, 1901), p. 56.

29 *Statutes of New College* (London, 1853), p. 68.

30 During term-time, a public sermon was preached here every Sunday morning, with exception of a few specified festivals, and days on which university masses were celebrated. See *Munim. acad.,* I, 289.

31 G. R. Owst, *Preaching in Medieval England* (Cambridge, 1926), p. 4.

32 *Dives and Pauper,* " Third command.", chap. 7.

33 The *Summa rudium,* written for simple folk of the fifteenth century,

and acts of penance[35] were suggested as laudable pursuits. Upon return from church, the layman was admonished to repeat the sermon to those of his household who had been unable to attend the service.[36] After meat, he was to engage in no idle sport, but to betake himself on errands of piety and mercy.[37] Particularly commendable were such practical manifestations of Christian virtue as almsgiving, visits to the sick, and the reconciliation of neighbors.[38] Whatever of the day remained before the ringing of the evensong bell might then be devoted to prayers, psalms, and the singing of hymns.[39]

Despite the fact that church services offered relief from monotonous toil, the peasant and the artisan sometimes preferred their humble tasks to the pious duties prescribed by clergymen of the stricter school. Manifestation of such inclinations was apt to provoke censure, however, for churchmen counted as servile agricultural and mechanical work, along with court proceedings and the business of buying and selling.[40] On the ground that labor of this sort distracted the mind and thus hindered a person from applying himself to things

shows how useful is the Sunday in enabling people who have been negligent about prayers and good works to make amends on that day. (" De tertio mandato"). In *Dives and Pauper* ("Third command.", chap. 19), Pauper says that Sunday was purposely appointed to give people opportunity to think of their own unkindnesses and God's great goodness.

34 Antoninus, *Summa*, II, tit. ix, c. 7, § 4; Clémanges, I, 147, col. 2.

35 Pilgrimages to near-by shrines were often undertaken for this reason.

36 J. Bromyard, *Summa predicantium* (Basel, 1487?), Pars I, art. 3, § ix, of the discussion entitled *Audire*.

37 Owst, *Preaching in Med. Eng.*, pp. 193-194.

38 *Dives and Pauper*, " Third command.", chap. 6. On holy days, especially, parents were admonished " to show their children the practical aspects of religion through almsgiving, the forgiveness of injuries, and other works of mercy." *Der Seelenführer*, printed in 1498, and quoted in J. Janssen, *Geschichte des deutschen Volkes seit dem Ausgang des Mittelalters* (Freiburg, 1896-1904), I, 34.

39 Alexander of Hales, Pars III, " Third command.", mem. v, art. 2; Henricus de Gorichem, fol. 12 r.

40 *Decret. Gregory IX*, Lib. II, tit. ix, c. 1.

of a divine nature, occupations in this category, in theory at least, were forbidden on Sundays and feast days.[41]

Inasmuch as the amount of rest allotted to servants, and even to animals, depended, in large measure, upon the judgment of masters, the injunction to hallow the holy day laid a double responsibility upon them.[42] Chaucer's allusion to the great sin done by folk who compelled their servants to toil out of time, as on holy days, suggests that they frequently showed no conscience about the matter.[43] Probably on the assumption that a man is concerned about that which touches his purse, Norwegian church law made a master liable for fines imposed upon his servants for holiday labor.[44] Provided the tasks were lawful in themselves, consensus of opinion granted exoneration to servants who, from a sense of duty, toiled at their master's bidding. If, on holy days, masters proved unreasonable in their demands, servants might justifiably refuse to fetch and carry at their behest.[45]

Opposed as they were to holiday labor, most churchmen concurred in St. Augustine's dictum that to engage in servile, albeit lawful, work on holy days was far less reprehensible than to pursue worldly pleasures.[46] As a salutary measure, therefore, St. Benedict stipulated in his *Rule* that those not disposed to read or to meditate on such occasions as Sunday, when these quiet occupations were especially enjoined, might pass the time in manual labor.[47] A matter of graver concern was the commis-

41 Astesanus de Asta, lib. I, tit. xxii; Henricus de Gorichem, fol. 10 r.

42 Raymond of Pennafort, *Summa*, tit. xii, § 2; *Dives and Pauper*, " Third command.", chaps. 8, 17; Henricus de Gorichem, fol. 13 r, prop. iv.

43 *Parson's Tale*, lines 667 f.

44 *Earliest Norweg. Laws*, p. 45, § 16; p. 237, § 28.

45 *Dives and Pauper*, " Third command.", chap. 17; Bernardino, II, 57, col. 2.

46 Henricus de Gorichem, fol. 14r, prop. vii; Alvarus Pelagius, Lib. II, art. xliii; Clémanges, I, 146, col. 2; and many others. All quote Augustine on this point.

47 Benedict of Nursia, *Regula monachorum*, edited by E. Woelfflin (Leipzig, 1895), cap. 48 (p. 50).

sion of sin on holidays, for then failure to hallow the day added weight to the transgression itself.[48] Mere obedience to the law, however, did not insure escape from censure, for almost as serious as overt acts were implied sins of the spirit. In the computation of such offenses preachers by no means limited themselves to shortcomings of the obvious sort. Bernardino of Siena went to such lengths that he included in his reckoning acts upon which the Old Testament had placed Sabbath interdiction. With medieval propensity for symbolism, he invested these prohibitions with allegorical significance. The burden-bearing forbidden by Scripture he interpreted as failure to renounce offenses toward God; the lighting of household fires, which was banned among the Hebrews, he construed as the sowing of discontent; and the gathering of wood, for which so heavy a penalty as death was once inflicted,[48a] he regarded as comparable to breaking the spirit with worldly thoughts.[49]

Fine distinctions drawn between that which was permissible and that which was forbidden on holy days depended, in large measure, upon an understanding of what constituted servile and non-servile employment. To considerations of this sort the *Summae confessorum* of the earlier period gave a good deal of attention. In discussing the matter, Astesano d'Asti (d. ca. 1330) shows how occupations which contribute to the good of the soul may be counted as liberal, despite their mechanical or servile appearance. Writing for purposes other than gain he cites as an example. On the contrary, works which pertain to the temporal good of the body must be reckoned as servile, even though they are sometimes masked under spiritual form. By way of further definition, Astesano resorts to the use of illus-

---

48 *Dives and Pauper,* " Third command.", chap. 7; Antoninus of Florence, *Summa,* pars II, tit. ix, c. 7, § 3. In support of this opinion, Bartholomeus Pisanus quotes (under *Ferie*) a comment of Nicolaus of Lyra on *Exodus,* XX: " He who commits a mortal sin on a feast day sins doubly, for he not only commits offense, but violates the sanctity of the day." Fines for misdeeds were higher on holy days. (*Corp. stat. ital.,* I, 148-149).

48a *Numbers,* XV, 32-36.

49 *Opera,* II, 55, col. 2-56, col. 1.

tration. If, on a holiday, a lawyer considers matters which he wishes to pursue with profit on the morrow, or a landlord lays plans for the next day's tillage of his fields, the effort involved in both instances is intellectual, yet, without doubt, the end in view is temporal gain. Under the heading of servile rather than free must therefore fall all such labor. Nevertheless, Astesano is inclined to believe that only in cases where work of this kind interferes with religious devotions is abstinence strictly enjoined.[50]

Whenever urgent need or pious cause arose, a person might procure exemption from the rule against Sunday and feast-day labor by applying to the proper ecclesiastical official.[51] If, at any time, an individual was puzzled about the legitimacy of such work, he did well to seek counsel, for, through too rigid or too lenient an interpretation of conscience, he might easily fall into error.[52] As a consultant, the bishop constituted the best of authorities,[53] but in case he were not at hand, one might profit by the advice of an honest priest,[54] or even that of an intelligent

50 *Summa*, lib. I, tit. xxii.

51 *Early Norweg. Laws*, p. 237, § 27. See also *Statuti dell'arte dei medici e speziali*, edited by R. Ciasca (Florence, 1925), p. 79. Even in cases of exemption, gild statutes sometimes stipulated that a part of the money earned through holiday work be given to the poor, or paid into a general fund, by way of compensation.

52 Angelus Carletus, fol. 128 r, § 35; Johannes Friburgensis, *Summa confessorum* (Augsburg, 1476), lib. I, tit. xii, quaest. viii; Bartholomeus Pisanus, art. "Ferie". In considering the observance of holy days, the University of Paris recognized the impossibility of regulating by rule situations pertaining to moral conduct, in which individual differences, customs of the region, and variety of circumstance play such a large part (*Chart. univ. Paris.*, IV, 460, § 15). Circumstances are the determining factor in such situations, says Alexander of Hales (pars III, quaest. 32, mem. iv). His point of view was, therefore, not unlike that of the Roman lawyer Scaevola, who, upon being asked what things might lawfully be done on holidays when work was forbidden, replied, "Anything, the omission of which would be injurious." Macrobius, *Saturnalia*, lib. I, c. 16, xi. See also Gerson, *Opera*, I, 432.

53 Johannes Friburgensis, lib. I, tit. xii, quaest. 8.

54 Bartholomeus Pisanus, art. "Ferie".

layman.[55] In the face of great emergency, a man might rely upon his own judgment, for, on occasion, necessity itself makes law.[56] It is not surprising that the difficulty of applying these general principles to the ordinary affairs of life troubled many people. At the beginning of his treatise on the celebration of holidays, the Carmelite Henry of Gorichem calls attention to the timeliness of such a discussion. Every day the subject raises practical questions concerning scruples of conscience, he says.[57] The frequency with which he was asked about the keeping of holy days led Francesco della Croce to set down some general rules regarding their observance.[58] His work may possibly have been hastened by the Sabbatarian tendencies of visiting friars, for the author makes casual reference to the dissatisfaction caused among poor folk by preachers' criticism of holiday labor.

Some activities commonly termed servile were sanctioned as necessitating an amount of labor too slight to hamper the freedom of the spirit in its devotion to God.[59] For the performance of such simple domestic tasks as a little sewing or sweeping, a housewife was therefore not to be censured,[60] nor was a farmer to be condemned if he pruned an injured vine,[61] or mended a break in ditch or hedge.[62] For this reason, it was also counted permissible for painters to apply gilt or varnish to works which were nearing completion.[63] Because comparatively little effort was involved, logs might be floated down-stream,[64] loaded

55 Baptista de Salis, fol. 218r, § 21.

56 Johannes Friburgensis, *loc. cit.*

57 *op. cit.*, fol. 10r.

58 *Tractatus de festis* (Milan, ? 1475 ?), [fol. 1 r.] The author was *primicerius* at the Cathedral of Milan in 1478.

59 Angelus Carletus, fol. 127 r, § 9.

60 *Idem.*

61 Bartholomeus Pisanus, art. " Ferie ".

62 *Idem.*

63 *Stat. dell'arte dei medici. . .*, p. 79.

64 *Early Norweg. Laws*, p. 240.

wagons might be brought home to shelter,[65] and burdens not too large for a man to carry might be transported with impunity.[66] There was strong disapproval of traffic as a whole, yet a single sale was not thought to imperil a shopkeeper's soul.[67]

Inasmuch as animals are entitled to a certain amount of rest, there was a general feeling that mills dependent upon horses or oxen for power ought not to be operated on holy days.[68] In regard to those run by wind or water, fewer restrictions prevailed.[69] In Paris, however, their operation during the time of church service was prohibited,[70] and Angelo Carletti di Chivasso thought that even windmills ought not to run unless there was actual need.[71] A practice similar to that which he recommended seems to have been followed in some north-Italian towns, for their statutes provide for the irrigation of land on holy days, when water was not used in the operation of mills.[72]

For pious purposes, servile labor on holy days was not only permissible, but was frankly marked with the stamp of approval. Caring for the destitute and wretched was always praiseworthy.[73] Laudable, too, was the lending of help to the poor in plowing and planting,[74] provided, of course, one did not omit mass, or work for the entire day, or to the point of

---

65 *Idem.*

66 *Ibid.*, p. 241.

67 Angelus Carletus, fol. 127v, §10.

68 Bartholomeus Pisanus, art. "Ferie".

69 Baptista de Salis, fol. 218 r, § 19. Angelus Carletus points out that a minimum of human effort is required for their operation (*op. cit.*, fol. 127 v, § 18).

70 E. Boileau, *Les métiers et corporations ... de Paris*, edited by R. de Lespinasse and F. Bonnardot (Paris, 1879), p. 16.

71 Angelus Carletus, fol. 127v, § 18.

72 *Corp. stat. ital.*, VI, 395 (st. xxiv) ; *ibid.*, X, 266 (st. clxxxv), and 257 (st. clix) ; *ibid.*, XV, 165 (st. lx).

73 *Dives and Pauper*, "Third command.", chap. 6; Baptista de Salis, 218r, § 21 ; Johannes Friburgensis, lib. I, tit. xii, quaest. 7.

74 Lyndwood, *Provinciale*, p. 101, and Gloss c on that page. See also Johannes Friburgensis, lib. I, tit. xii, quaest.11.

fatigue.[75] To the rendering of such aid on major festivals, Bartolomeo Pisano,[76] and John of Freiburg [77] were opposed; representative of a more general opinion, however, was the contention of Angelo Carletti di Chivasso that works of piety and compassion know neither time nor season.[78] Arranging terms of peace [79] and repairing roads and bridges [80] were considered employments well suited to holidays, for to the medieval mind public utility constituted one of the manifold aspects of piety.[81] Carting of wood and stone for the building or mending of church and monastery was deemed meritorious,[82] if it was done without the hope of reward.[83] Entirely permissible were the sale of candles for church purposes [84] and the conveyance of pilgrims by land or by water.[85]

Much servile labor on holidays was countenanced on the ground of necessity. Under works which did not permit postponement fell the feeding of stock,[86] the care of meat in sum-

75 Monaldus, *Summa*, fol. 76 r, col. 1.

76 *Summa*, see " Ferie ".

77 *loc. cit.*

78 *Summa*, fol. 128r, § 28; Durandus, *Speculum*, II, fol. 60 v.

79 Hostiensis, col. 515.

80 Baptista de Salis, fol. 217 v, § 15. At a somewhat later period (1577), a certain Thomas Gibbs, summoned to the archdeacon's court for violation of the Sunday, offered as excuse the obligation to replace a footbridge stolen during the night. Since church-goers had openly complained that they could not make their way in safety because of the lack of a crossing, he had, during service-time, felled a tree and built a bridge thereof. Hale, *Preced. and Proceed. . . from Act-books of Eccl. Courts,* p. 165.

81 Angelus Carletus, fol. 128r, § 32.

82 Monaldus, fol. 76r, col. 1.

83 Angelus Carletus, fol. 128r, § 28. The author of *Dives and Pauper* was inclined to think that men who could afford to pay for cartage on week-days were not excused if they spent the holy day in this fashion. " Third command.", chap. 16.

84 E. Rodocanachi, *Corporations ouvrières à Rome depuis la chute de l'empire romain* (Paris, 1894), II, 394, art. 62.

85 Johannes Friburgensis, lib. I, tit. xii, quaest. 9.

86 Thomas Aquinas, pars II, II, quaest. 122, art. 4; *Early Norweg. Laws*, p. 238, § 30.

mer,[87] the repair of a house to prevent its ruin,[88] and the unloading of cargo likely to be damaged by water, or lost through dispersal.[89] Since provision for an adequate food supply constituted a problem of major importance throughout the Middle Ages, it was generally understood that holy days presented no obstacle to the harvesting of crops endangered by the approach of a storm,[90] the imminence of a flood,[91] or the advance of an enemy.[92] About the genuineness of the menace, however, there was to be no doubt.[93] In countries like Norway, where agricultural supplies were limited, it was imperative that men should fish in season, without regard to feast or festival. Alexander III had therefore granted fisherfolk permission to take advantage of the running of the herring.[94] By way of compensation, it was stipulated that a portion of the holiday catch be set aside for the poor.[95] In cases where men were forced by actual poverty to work on holy days to support themselves and their families, the Church adopted a policy of understanding.[96] In such circumstances it was suggested, however, that dispensation be sought from the bishop.[97]

Because the cooking of food was seen to contribute to the preservation of health, preparations of that sort were not sub-

87 Angelus Carletus, fol. 127 v, § 11.

88 *Ibid.*, fol. 128 r, § 24.

89 *Early Norweg. Laws,* p. 241, § 36; *Corp. stat. ital.,* III, 173 (stat. cxxix).

90 Johannes Friburgensis, lib. I, tit. xii, quaest. 9.

91 *Idem.*

92 *Ibid.,* quaest. 7.

93 Bernardino of Siena criticizes those who do not act in good faith; he reminds them that God questions the heart, not the hand. Forethought and good management would sometimes obviate use of the holy day for such purposes. See *Opera*, II, 58, col. 2.

94 *Early Norweg. Laws,* p. 236, § 26.

95 *Ibid.,* p. 237, § 27.

96 Lyndwood, *Provinciale,* p. 101; *Piers Plowman,* C XIV, lines 82-86; Johannes Friburgensis, lib. I, tit. xii, quaest. 11.

97 Antoninus, *Summa,* pars II, tit. ix, c. 7 (col. 987).

ject to Sunday or feast-day restrictions.[98] Attention directed by one person to the bodily well-being of another was also considered in no way contrary to the observance of the most solemn of festivals, inasmuch as Christ had not hesitated to heal the sick on the Sabbath. On such grounds Thomas Aquinas justified the care of physicians for patients.[99] Of much greater importance than the bodily safety of an individual, however, was the safe-guarding of the common weal. To prevent loss of life and the destruction of property, war waged in self-defense not only received sanction, but was regarded almost as a moral obligation. Hence erection of fortifications, the digging of trenches, the manufacture of missiles, and the transportation of things essential to the defense were counted permissible under threat of attack. It was, of course, understood that all such activities should cease with the passage of danger.[100]

Unusual circumstance or a sense of obligation toward persons in distress often necessitated holiday labor for which due allowance was made. In well-regulated cities like Florence, difficulty in purchasing drugs for the sick was obviated by the provision that on holy days apothecaries serve the public in turn [101]—but only at the wicket, in recognition of the sanctity of the day.[102] At Rome, where we should expect to find church festivals marked by strict observance, clothmakers were permitted to sell black fabrics to individuals suddenly plunged into mourning.[103] and bankers might legitimately transact business till noon on Easter Monday, in order that pilgrims on the verge of departure might obtain money for their homeward jour-

98 Alexander of Hales, pars III, quaest. 32, mem. v.

99 Thomas Aquinas, pars II, II, quaest. 40, art. 4.

100 The example of the Maccabees furnished a precedent. To refrain from fighting in self-defense would be " tempting God ", according to Thomas Aquinas (*Summa theologica*, pars II, II, quaest. 40, art. 4).

101 Antoninus, *Summa*, pars III, tit. viii, c. 4, § 6; see also Bernardino of Siena, *Opera*, III, 265, col. 1.

102 *Statuti dell'arte dei medici e speziali*, p. 44.

103 *Statuti dei mercanti di Roma*, edited by G. Gatti (Rome, 1885), 52, 80.

ney.[104] Although innkeepers frequently incurred clerical condemnation for furnishing meat and drink to villagers on Sundays and saints' days,[105] they were supposed to offer hospitality
to wayfarers upon all occasions.[106] Within their dwellings, London girdlers might lawfully sell their wares on feast days to any
stranger who had reason to make a hasty purchase on his way
through the city,[107] and farriers might honestly ply their trade
for the accommodation of a traveller whose horse had lost
a shoe.[108]

Toward the matter of holiday travel itself, most churchmen
were inclined to adopt a liberal attitude, on the ground that
ambling or trudging along the road did not necessarily interfere with meditation or the contemplation of things divine.[109]
To those desirous of having scriptural basis for their views, the
obvious inclusion of the Sabbath in the seven days' march
around Jericho, and Elijah's forty-day journey in the wilder-
ness furnished satisfactory evidence.[110] When discharge of
clerical duties or some pious motive accounted for the under-
taking of a journey, no question of its legitimacy arose.[111] For
any number of reasons it became apparent that often Sunday

104 Rodocanachi, *op. cit.*, I, ciii; II, 12

105 In some places food and drink were not to be sold until after mass.
Records of the Borough of Northampton, edited by C. A. Markham . . .
and J. C. Cox (London, etc., 1898), I, 311.

106 Angelus Carletus, fol. 127v, § 12; Rodocanachi, *op. cit.,* I, xxv;
Records of . . . Northampton, I, 311.

107 Riley, *Mem. of London,* p. 217.

108 Rodocanachi, *op. cit.,* I, xxxv; *Statuti della Repubblica Fiorentina,*
II, 398, c. 56; *Corp. stat. ital.,* XIII, 223.

109 Angelus Carletus, fol. 127v, § 15.

110 Alexander of Hales, in his *Summa* (pars III, quaest. 32, mem. iv,
quotes John of Damascus on this point.

111 *Dives and Pauper,* "Third command.", chap. 16. For the sake of
example, Bernardino of Siena feels that clergymen ought not to travel on
holy days without good reason (*Opera,* II, 57, col. 2). Statutes of the
Fullers' Gild of Lincoln stipulated that a member setting out, on a Sunday
or a feast day, upon a pilgrimage to Rome, was to be accompanied without the city by his fellowcraftsmen, who were to speed him on his way. See
Smith, *English Gilds,* p. 180.

or feast day travel could not be avoided. Messengers and couriers, for example, were obliged to continue on their way,[112] and carriers who had received commissions to remote localities, frequently could not, without serious inconvenience, delay their return beyond the holy day.[113] In cases of actual necessity, tenants who owed grain-carriage duty to their lords were permitted to fulfill the obligation;[114] they fell into grievous error, however, if they rendered this service on holidays for the sole purpose of being free at other times to work for themselves.[115] Needless travel on holidays and feast days Antonino of Florence viewed with disfavor.[116] In fact, he was of the opinion that one should forego a day's journey unless force of circumstance or the performance of some pious task impelled one to take to the road. In a visit to a shrine, the obtaining of an indulgence, or an attempt to remove the taint of scandal, he found motives to which he could give his approval. Regardless of the importance of the mission, he felt that one should attend the service of the mass, if possible, and refrain from traveling to the point of exhaustion.[117]

In determining what legal activities were to be sanctioned on holy days, canonists, in their interpretation of church law, followed closely the regulations set down in the *Corpus iuris civilis* concerning holidays.[118] Such voluntary acts as the emancipation of a son or the manumission of a slave were fully sanctioned,[119] and the drawing of marriage contracts on holy days was countenanced in districts where a custom of this sort pre-

112 Baptista de Salis, fol. 128r, col. 2, § 20.

113 *Astesanus de Asta*, lib. I, tit. xxiii.

114 Angelus Carletus, fol. 127v, § 20; Bartholomeus Pisanus, *op. cit.*, "Ferie".

115 Johannes Friburgensis, lib. I, tit. xii, quaest. 9; Astesanus de Asta, lib. I, tit. xxiii.

116 Antoninus, *Summa*, pars II, tit. ix, c. 7, § 5; *Dives and Pauper*, "Third command.", chap. 16. Pauper also thinks it a grievous error to make a practice of Sunday travel, unless there is great need.

117 Antoninus, *op. cit.*

118 *Supra*, chap. 1, n. 34.

119 Hostiensis, col. 515; Baptista de Salis, fol. 218r, col. 2, § 21.

vailed.[120] In both theory and practice, critical illness, or a desire to bestow goods upon the Church, served on such occasion as ample justification for the making of wills [121] and the conveyance of property by deed.[122] Truces might honestly be arranged,[123] oaths pertaining to the establishment of peace might be administered at all times,[124] and cases involving the destitute and wretched were seen to brook no delay.[125] Whenever circumstances warranted, orders for the maintenance of parents or children might be issued,[126] and the appointment of guardians and trustees was always permissible.[127] In cases of injury or theft, or disasters such as fire and shipwreck, where lapse of time might easily render the object of the proceedings useless, it was considered proper for investigations to be undertaken at once.[128] Even on feast days of major importance, a person suspected of wrongdoing might legitimately be taken into custody, if he were thought to be contemplating flight.[129] Under no circumstances was the care of prisoners to be neglected,[130] or were officers to be hampered in their administration of military discipline.[131] Whenever a situation demanding immediate attention arose, university rectors, too, might proceed in disci-

120 Antoninus, *Summa*, pars II, tit. ix, c. 7, § 5.

121 *Idem;* see also Durandus, *Speculum*, II, fol. 60v.

122 *Statuti di Bellano e Mandello,* edited by E. Anderloni and V. Adami (Milan, 1932), p. 280.

123 Hostiensis, col. 515; see also Franciscus de Cruce, *Tract. de festis* [fol. 5 v].

124 Azo of Bologna, *Summa aurea* (Lyons, 1557), "De feriis", fol. 46v, col. 2. Some business pertaining to the commune might also be transacted; see *Corp. stat. ital.*, XIII, 101 (rub. 4).

125 Durandus, *Speculum*, II, fol. 60v; Hostiensis, col. 515; *Corp. stat. ital.*, II, 177 (stat. 19).

126 Azo, *loc. cit.*

127 *Idem.*

128 *Idem;* also *Stat. della Repub. Fiorentina*, II, 111 (rub. 34).

129 *Corp. stat. ital.*, VIII, 223 (stat. 141); *Stat. di. . . . Mandello*, pp. 330-31 (stat. 325); Bartolus de Saxoferrato, *Commentaria*, VII, 99v, col. 2.

130 Azo, fol. 46v, col. 2.

131 Hostiensis, col. 515.

plinary cases on holidays, with the possible exception of a few especially solemn ones.[132] In recognition of the fact that clients who came from a distance might be seriously inconvenienced by the intervention of a holy day of local significance, advocates were granted the right of offering them counsel.[133] In such instances, the sixteenth-century canonist Pierre Rebuffi (1487-1557), maintained that necessity lent sanction to that which, under ordinary circumstances, was forbidden.[134] Although fees for such services might be accepted, it was generally understood that compensation was not to be considered an end in itself. In Rebuffi's opinion, no lawyer could pursue a more exemplary policy than that adopted by Joannes Boerius, a jurist of Montpellier : from the throng of clients who sought his advice, he made a practice of giving his attention, on holidays, only to the poor.[135]

Despite the exactness of the duties prescribed by the Church for Sundays and saints' days, churchmen were not entirely unmindful of the importance of employing these occasions for the refreshment of body and mind.[136] In his discussion of the

132 *Stat.... delle studio bolognese*, p. 12. See also P. Rebuffi, " De privilegiis scholarium," *Tractatus illustrium in utraque tum pontificii, tum caesarei iuris facultate iurisconsultorum*, XVIII, fol. 34r, col. 1, § 1. Here Hostiensis and Panormitanus (Nicolaus de Tudeschis) are given as authorities.

133 The inconvenience of local holidays is to be seen in one of the stereotyped situations described in a treatise on the " court baron ". The presiding officer asks of the defendant :
" Bernard of G, art thou come here with thy law to acquit thee that thou didst not slay my lord's pig?"
" Nay, sir, I cannot have the folk ready here at this day, for that they are at the feast of [some other village]."
" What wilt thou give to have respite to another court?"
" A bezant of gold, sir."
" Then we assess thee a day at the next court."
See *The Court Baron, being Precedents for Use in Seignorial and Other Local Courts, ...* edited by F. W. Maitland and W. P. Baildon (London, 1891), pp. 56-57.

134 Rebuffi, *op. cit.*, XVIII, fol. 33r, col. 2, § 20.

135 *Ibid.*, fol. 33v, col. 1, § 20.

136 *Dives and Pauper,* " Third command.", chap. 17.

third commandment, Gerson, for example, makes the statement that recreations like walking, and honest sport for the sake of enjoyment, are especially desirable at such times.[137] It is possible that the eminent theologian did not endorse these pastimes wholeheartedly but merely looked upon them as the lesser of two evils, for he hastens to add that, through injudicious eating and drinking, through dancing and participation in games of an objectionable sort, one might easily fall into sin on holy days.[138] Antonino of Florence also approved of recreation of the proper kind. Athletic games he considered suitable forms of diversion, although he would have one remember that some sports like casting the stone are not only perilous in themselves, but dangerous because of the boisterousness of their character.[139] Such pastimes as running, wrestling, and throwing the javelin, were acceptable to the Dominican Bartolomeo Pisano, for these activities he counted beneficial to the body.[140] In his description of London in the twelfth century, William Fitzstephen mentions these exercises, along with archery, as favorite sports of his day.[141] By the close of the fourteenth century the popularity of casting the stone, for example, had not waned, for John Mirk, Prior of Lilleshall, speaks of it as one of the forms of amusement not to be enjoyed within the churchyard.[142] To the list of " importunate " games in which people indulged on holidays, a statute of Richard II adds quoits, skittles, football, and tennis.[143] Churchmen probably manifested little enthusiasm for some of the pastimes that are said by Fitzstephen to have been associated with certain seasons of the year—mimic warfare of youths on Sundays in Lent,[144] quintain games on the river at Easter-time,[145] and cockfighting at Shrovetide.[146] This last diversion, along with the form of revelry picturesquely

---

137 *Opera*, I, 432.

138 *Ibid.*, I, 432-433.

139 *Summa*, II, tit. 1, c. 23, § i.

140 See the section entitled *Ludi*.

141 " Description of London ", *Liber custumarum*, I, chap. 21.

142 *Instr. for Parish Priests*, lines 330-337.

143 12 Richard II, c. 6.

144 Fitzstephen, *op. cit.*, chap. 19.

145 *Ibid.*, chap. 20.

146 *Ibid.*, chap. 18.

known as the " rydyng aboute of victory ",[146a] Colet had sternly forbidden by statute when he founded his school at St. Paul's.[147] Yet at Scottish universities cockfighting proved such a popular amusement that a two or three-day vacation at carnival-time was granted for this express purpose.[148] The Church had never approved of Sunday and holiday jousts and tourneys, which offered such irresistible attraction to students at Heidelberg [149] and Leipzig; [150] consequently these spectacles were denounced in no uncertain terms by eloquent preachers.[151] If engaged in purely for recreation, hunting, fowling, and fishing were regarded as lawful holiday activities.[152] In the opinion of some practical-minded prelates, these pursuits were unusually satisfactory pastimes, for they not only furnished diversion,[153] but also served a useful end, if a man chanced to be an adept angler or hunter.[154] Unfortunately these recreations were frequently enjoyed at a lord's expense, for while good Christian folk were at church hearing mass, conscienceless sportsmen were wont to roam through his parks or to encroach upon his preserves.[155]

It must not be forgotten that, in the Middle Ages, a number of games which seem harmless in themselves met with general

146a J. Strutt, *Sports and Pastimes of the People of England* (London, 1845), pp. 394-95. This sport seems to have consisted in carrying on a long pole the boy who had won a cock, or whose cock had come off victorious.

147 J. Lupton, *Life of John Colet* (London, 1887), p. 166.

148 H. Rashdall, *Universities of Europe in the Middle Ages* (Oxford, 1936), III, 423.

149 E. Winkelmann, *Urkundenbuch der Universität Heidelberg* (Heidelberg, 1886), I, 171. A conversation designed to discourage an interest in jousts and tournaments is to be found in the *Manuale scholarium,* translated by R. F. Seybolt (Cambridge, Mass., 1921), p. 101.

150 *Die Statutenbücher der Universität Leipzig,* edited by F. Zarncke, (Leipzig, 1861), p. 111.

151 Silvestro Mazzolini da Prierio, *Summa summarum* (Lyons, 1528), art. "Ludus", fol. 98v; see also Bromyard, *op. cit.,* art. "Ludus".

152 Baptista de Salis, fol. 217v, col. 1, § 11.

153 Antoninus of Florence, *Summa,* pars III, tit. viii, c. 4, § 13.

154 Baptista de Salis, *loc. cit.*

155 13 Richard II, stat. 1, c. 13.

disapproval,[156] because they tended to encourage such vices as blasphemy,[157] perjury,[158] and deceit,[159] and not infrequently provoked quarrels which, in extreme cases, resulted in the actual shedding of blood.[160] Especially to be frowned upon were dicing and other games of chance, for in this fashion men often wasted their substance, and suddenly found themselves reduced to poverty.[161] In some localities, during the Christmas season, when considerable license was countenanced, this type of diversion was permitted in manor house [162] and college hall.[163] Pronounced

156 *Handlyng Synne*, lines 985-986; Mirk, *Instr. for Par. Priests*, lines 997 ff.

157 *Summa rudium*, "De secundo mandato."

158 Bartholomaeus Pisanus, *Summa*, art. "Ludi"; see also Mazzolini, *loc. cit.*

159 *Idem.*

160 Grosseteste complained that games often provoked anger, hatred, brawls, and even homicides. (*Epistolae*, edited by H. R. Luard [London, 1861], p. 74). In the *Visitations of Southwell Minster* it is noted that "Dominus Ricardus Gurnell multitotiens per totum annum ludit ad cartas cum laicis ut per hujusmodi ludum dissensiones oriuntur et contumeliae, et fere de verisimili timetur de homicidio" (see pp. 46-47).

161 *Decameron*, IX, 4, represents an extreme case. Fortarrigo not only gambled away everything that he had, down to his very clothes, but having helped himself to the purse of his namesake and companion, he lost that too, and so was left with nothing except the shirt in which he stood.

162 H. T. Riley, *Memorials of London and London Life in the XIIIth, XIVth, and XVth Centuries* (London, 1868), p. 193; J. Stow, *A Survey of London*, edited by W. J. Thomas (London, 1842), p. 37.

163 *Stat. . . . dello studio bolognese*, p. 292, rub. 99. At Brasenose College, Oxford, cards were permitted at Christmas at the discretion of the principal. (*Stats.*, p. 27, c. 23). At St. John's College, Cambridge, fellows, but not scholars, might play at dice and cards, provided they did so in the hall, for recreation only, and not far into the night. (*Early Stats.* of the College, p. 138, c. 26). At Heidelberg, however, no *ludi taxillorum* were allowed at this time. In order that ignorance might not be offered as ground for excuse, it was stipulated that the prohibitory statute be read each year before the beginning of the Christmas season. (Winkelmann, I, 15). For other regulations regarding dicing and games of chance, see Rashdall, *Univ. of Europe*, III, 420-21.

fondness for gambling in districts of southern Europe led to the granting of this indulgence at Easter-time too.[164]

Numerous denunciations in contemporary sermons attest the popularity of dancing [165] and dramatic performances [166] as holiday attractions. Condemnation did not represent the attitude of all churchmen, however. In the *Dialogue of Dives and Pauper* a more rational point of view is to be found in Pauper's contention that mirth-making on holidays lies quite within the law, since the holy day was ordained for rest and the refreshment of body and soul. When Christian folk were closely associated with heathen people, there was grave danger of their being affected by the objectionable character of the latter's amusements. St. Augustine's disapproval of dancing and theatrical productions he therefore attributes to the evils of a bygone age. While he maintains that all holiday pastimes conducive to sloth, gluttony, and idleness on workdays are unlawful at all times, he feels confident that St. Augustine did not intend his criticism to apply to honest dances and plays done in good manner and due season on the holy day.[167] With heresy afoot, it is not surprising that Pauper expresses the pious hope that errors against the faith of Holy Church would not creep into these plays. Of the liturgical drama he thinks especially well. The presentation of Herod and the Three Kings at Christmas-tide, and the portrayal of biblical incidents on Easter and other great festivals, he finds commendable, for some men can only be reached through ' gamen and play '.[168]

164 *Corp. stat. ital.*, III, 121, c. 57; *Stat. di Bellano . . .*, pp. 22, c. 8; 46, c. 59.

165 *Anec. hist. . . . d'Étienne de Bourbon*, pp. 168, 397. See also Jacques de Vitry, *Exempla*, pp. 114, 131. As an illustration of the contrast between the tenor of the early fifteenth century and that of St. Augustine's time, Nicolas de Clémanges uses the popular attitude toward dancing. Formerly, this sort of amusement was condemned, but in his own day, Clémanges finds that he who treads the intricate measures of the dance receives nothing but approval. Clémanges, I, 146, col. 2.

166 J. Bromyard, *Summa predicantium*, art. "Ludi".

167 "Third command.", chap. 17.

168 *Idem.*

University authorities were less inclined to entertain such liberal views. Since a great many students were clerks, it was thought unfitting for them to attend dramatic performances in public places.[169] Too often pageants, even those presented in churches, were undignified and somewhat jesting in tone. If, however, suitable ones could be found, the statutes of some colleges stated that, for the sake of recreation, students might tarry for a short time.[170] In the maskings and disguisings so universally popular at Christmas-tide in England, France, and other countries of western Europe, even austere disciplinarians like Wykeham[171] and Colet[172] allotted students a share in the election of the Boy Bishop, the Lord of Misrule, or the King of Christmas, known at Merton College as the *Rex Fabarum*.[173] Inversion of status, which prevailed during the reign of these potentates, must have been a source of much amusement to youths whose high spirits often had their only outlet in what Rashdall calls " ecclesiastical dissipation ".[174] Various forms of entertainment were provided by these temporary officers, who presided over the festivities of this season. The Boy Bishop sometimes gave a dinner to clerks and choir boys before setting out with his retinue to visit houses in the neighborhood,[175] and the *Rex Fabarum* was wont to treat his companions with wine and capon, and to furnish an evening fire and many jests (*cum multis farculis*) for the pleasure of his guests.[176]

169 St. Peter's College, Statutes of 1344, *Documents Relating to the University and Colleges of Cambridge* (London, 1852), II, 31.

170 *Idem.*

171 " Stats. of New College ", p. 69. At a somewhat later period, Bishop Ponet, in a controversy with Thomas Martin, charged his opponent with having learned his boldness while playing minion to the Christmas lord at New College, Oxford. See Ponet, *An Apologie*, pp. 14-15.

172 Lupton, *Life of Colet*, p. 278.

173 *Registrum annalium collegii Mertonensis*, 1483-1521, edited by H. E. Salter (Oxford, 1923), pp. xviii-xix, 70, 94, 104, 118.

174 *Univ. of Europe*, III, 423.

175 K. Young, *The Drama of the Medieval Church* (Oxford, 1933), I, 109.

176 *Reg. annal. coll. Merton.*, pp. 260, 287.

Within the precincts of the university itself, plays were unwelcome until a relatively late period.[177] Mimes and farces were considered inappropriate diversions for occasions as gala as the feasts of St. Catherine and St. Nicholas,[178] or the days celebrated in honor of the patron saints of nations or provinces.[179] For similar festivals, even comedies which appeared in the form of moralities were frowned upon by academic authorities, who thought them far too distracting, too expensive, and too provocative of rivalry and scandal to be desirable amusement.[180] Modest holiday entertainment befitting the clerical state was provided in college halls, where groups of students might gather about the fire to listen to chronicles of the realm, recount marvels of the world, or sing carols.[181] Conversation in the vernacular was permitted at such times,[182] and additional allowance for commons was made on the greater festivals.[183]

Toward the close of the Middle Ages the prejudice against plays seems to have been set aside temporarily during the Christmas holidays. Oxford expense books of the latter part of the fifteenth century list expenditures for dramatic performances at this season,[184] and at Merton College gay interludes sometimes furnished entertainment for the " regents' fire," which was celebrated in the hall at the end of January,[185] and so virtually marked the close of this hilarious period, which is said to

177 F. S. Boas, *University Drama in the Tudor Age* (Oxford, 1914), pp. 2 ff.

178 (Stats, of Perpignan), Fournier, II, 674, § 35.

179 (Stats. of Orleans), Fournier, I, 218, § 13. See also *Chart. univ. Paris.*, IV, 730 (No. 2690).

180 Stats. of Orleans), Fournier, I, 218, § 13.

181 *Stat. of the Colleges of Oxford:* All Soul's Coll., pp. 35-36; Corpus Christi Coll., p. 80; Cardinal Coll., p. 98; King's Coll., Cambridge, *Doc. of Cambr. Univ.*, II, 532-533.

182 *Statuta antiqua universitatis Oxoniensis*, edited by S. Gibson (Oxford, 1931), p. 579.

183 *Codice diplomatico dell' università di Pavia*, edited by R. Maiocchi (Pavia, 1905-1915), II, 257, 366.

184 See Boas, *Univ. Drama in the Tudor Age*, pp. 2 ff.

185 *Reg. annal. coll. Merton.*, pp. 260, 287, 434.

have extended to Candlemas.[186] In 1488, at the University of Paris, rather reluctant permission was granted by authorities of the Faculty of Arts for the giving of one or, at most, two mimes at the time of the Feast of Kings.[187] In conformity with regulations, these performances took place on the vigil of the holiday or after vespers on the day itself, so that they might detract in no way from the devotion with which the feast proper was to be observed. According to stipulations, these plays were not to be elaborate affairs, although, in deference to the king and his lords, coverings might be placed on their seats, and rich stuffs might be used in cases where the station of the characters required them. Mindful of the proverbial poverty of students, authorities forbade the levying of sums to defray the cost of production and thoughtfully provided for expenses with money drawn from a general fund. Before presentation, a college official, or his representative, was to visit the plays to see that the comic portions contained no sarcastic or objectionable features. Repeated admonitions against borrowing of costumes and properties, which these measures include, remind one of the dire consequences that sometimes result from such a practice. Matthew Paris tells the story of a Norman clerk, Geoffrey of Le Mans, who took the habit as penance for his carelessness in allowing the choir copes and other articles which he had borrowed from the monastery of St. Albans for his school play, *The Miracle of St. Katharine*, to be burned along with his house.[188]

Since stern disciplinarians were wont to regard leisure and pleasure as two of " the ancient enemy's " most powerful weapons,[189] they were predisposed to look upon intellectual, and hence non-servile, activities like reading and studying as permissible holiday occupations.[190] To be sure, examination of the

186 J. Stow, *Survey of London* (Thoms ed.), p. 37, col. 2.

187 Du Boulay, *Hist. univ. Paris.*, V, 782-83.

188 T. Walsingham, *Gesta abbatum S. Albani,* edited by H. T. Riley (London, 1867), I, 73.

189 (Stat. of Perpignan), Fournier, II, 673.

190 Baptista de Salis, fol. 217 v, col. 1, § 9.

Scriptures offered the most fruitful field of endeavor,[191] but subjects like theology and canon law, which served to honor God and to promote the public good, were also of great value.[192] It would, of course, be a mistake to assume that necromancy or any other forbidden branch of knowledge could be considered a legitimate pursuit at any time.[193] For those in holy orders, *fabulae turpes* and *libri amatorii* were also thought unsuitable reading.[194] Disapproval of the classics is humorously shown in the *Letters of Obscure Men* by an old master's contention that, at Leipzig, a candidate had once been rejected because one of the examiners had found him reading Terence on a feast day.[195] Clerks to whom volumes of this sort proved an irresistible temptation were bidden to profit by Jerome's example and to foreswear the works of classical authors.[196] Needless to say, study was to interfere in no way with church attendance,[197] nor was it to be pursued for mercenary reasons.[198] In the case of doctors and lawyers, whose studies were likely to lie along professional lines and so to be conducted principally for gain, there was grave doubt as to their legitimacy.[199] Even under such conditions, however, the consensus of opinion conceded them to be more desirable holiday employment than playing at hazards or other equally objectionable games.

University holidays were numerous and apparently popular, for should no feast day recognized by academic authorities occur within the week, the statutes of Bologna,[200] Montpellier,[201]

191 Clémanges, I, 156, col. 1.   192 Angelus Carletus, fol. 128 r, § 29.

193 Rebuffi, *Tractatus illustrium ... iurisconsultorum*, XVIII, fol. 33 v, col. 1, § 21; Wyclif (?), *Of the Leaven of Pharisees*, pp. 8-9.

194 Rebuffi, *loc. cit.*

195 *Epistolae obscurorum virorum*, edited by F. G. Stokes (London, 1909), p. 486.

196 Rebuffi, *loc. cit.*

197 From the complaints of theologians, it is safe to assume that it did. See Alvarus Pelagius, lib. II, fol. 140 v, art. 29.

198 Angelus Carletus, fol. 128 r, § 29.

199 Rebuffi, *op. cit.*, XVIII, fol. 33 r, col. 2, § 20.

200 *Stat. ... dello studio bolognese*, p. 101.

201 *Cart. de Montpellier* (Stat. de l'Univ. de Med.), I, 350, § 32.

Perpignan,[202] and Poitiers [203] stipulated that Wednesday or Thursday should be set aside as a holiday. It seems unlikely that this expedient could have been resorted to frequently at Montpellier, since the statutes of its University of Law, in 1339, listed seventy-seven feast days which were to be observed, in addition to the Sundays of the year.[204] Church services, elaborate as they sometimes were,[205] did not usually take up the entire holiday. From the disapproval of idleness and sport expressed in university statutes, it is manifest that a student was not at liberty to spend the remainder of the day in such fashion.[206] Occupations suitable to the leisure hours which holy days afforded were, however, more numerous than might be supposed. The library was officially closed, but if a young man wished very much to continue his reading there, a knock at the door and the good offices of the librarian might gain him admission.[207] He might also read in his room,[208] if, like Chaucer's Clerk, he were

202 Fournier, II, 674, § 17.

203 (Univ. of Poitiers, Fac. of Law—Stat. of 1504), Fournier, III, 334, § 8.

204 *Cart. de Montpellier,* I, 311-312.

205 At Angers, the *pedagogus* was instructed to send students off to church before breakfast *(ante tentaculum),* and to see that they attended mass, and any other services which the character of the day required (Fournier, I, 432, § 126). Masters and doctors were also required to attend, in order to serve as a good example to students (Stat. of Univ. of Vienna, Kink, II, 76). Students were to see that their church manners were beyond reproach (Stat. of the Univ. of Toulouse, Fournier, I, 711). For other statutes regarding church attendance, see *Cart. de Montpellier,* I, 303, 341; Fournier, III, 165, § 26 (Univ. of Caen); *Cod. diplom. . . . di Pavia,* II, 368, 373; *Stat. of the Colleges of Oxford:* Oriel Coll., p. 15; Brasenose Coll., p. 18; Balliol Coll., p. 9; Exeter Coll., p. 309; Magdalen Coll., p. 63.

206 On Sunday, ecclesiastical obligations replaced the usual scholastic ones (*Stat. of Queen's Coll., Oxford,* pp. 28-29). The basis for this requirement is sometimes set forth in the statutes. Those of Christ's College, Cambridge, state: "Nothing is more to be avoided by a young man than slothful idleness. And on this account we will and appoint that each pupil shall always, as far as is possible, be occupied either in the worship of God, or in the study of the liberal arts, or in learning virtuous manners." *Docs. rel. to the Univ. of Cambr.,* III, 205.

207 Fournier, I, 387, §§ 7, 8.

208 Rebuffi, *op. cit.,* XVIII, fol. 33 r, col. 2, § 17.

fortunate enough to own several volumes, or were enrolled in the law school, where a few text-books seem to have been required. Since intellectual work was a lawful holiday pursuit, he might even employ his time in writing a sermon,[209] or in composing verses or letters on literary subjects.[210] He might also transcribe lecture notes, particularly those which he could not easily commit to memory in any other way.[211] A fine manuscript hand, or a desire to increase his allowance, should not, however, tempt a student to spend a feast day in the mere mechanical copying of a large work. Such procedure was sure to be looked upon with disfavor,[212] although, in the opinion of some authorities, this objection might be waived if the material was of a spiritual nature.[213]

Although by no means uniform regulations prevailed, Sundays and festivals enjoined upon the church as a whole were listed as " non-legible " days in the calendars of most institutions.[214] At these times doctors and masters customarily refrained from regular lecturing,[215] since their courses were prescribed and carried salary or fees.[216] Failure to conform to this practice called forth condemnation from the pulpit. Gautier de Chateau-Thierry, a thirteenth-century preacher, speaks with amazement of masters who, for silver, lecture even on Sundays and holy days, times when, for the welfare of their souls, they should endeavor to set a good example to the laity.[217] Bachelors and students, whose discourses no one felt obliged to attend, might lecture on all but festivals of highest rank,[218] for by

209 Johannes Friburgensis, lib. I, tit. xii, quaest. 9.

210 *Stat. Corpus Christi Coll.*, pp. 56-57.

211 Johannes Friburgensis, *loc. cit.*

212 Bartolomaeus Pisanus, art. " Ferie "; Angelus Carletus, fol. 128 r, § 31.

213 *Ibid.*, fol. 128 r, §§ 29, 31.

214 See *Munim. acad.* (Oxford), I, cxxxix ff; *Chart. univ. Paris.*, II, 709 ff; etc.

215 Kink, II, 129.

216 Baptista de Salis, 217 v, col. 1, § 10.

217 C. H. Haskins, *Studies in Medieval Culture* (Oxford, 1929), p. 55.

218 *Stat.... dello studio bolognese*, p. 101.

these exercises they presumably learned rather than taught.[219] By the fifteenth century the attitude of practical-minded Italians toward the acceptance of salary for this type of service seems to have grown more liberal. At Pavia, for instance, salaries were attached to various series of holiday lectures,[220] and at Pisa sums were even paid to students lecturing on festivals [221] —a medieval equivalent to the granting of scholarships, perhaps. Despite this change in point of view, Antonino of Florence still felt that masters ought not to accept fees from their students for this sort of lecture if they had other means of support.[222]

Saints' days, other than those of major importance, were considered excellent times for disputation,[223] a form of exercise far more acceptable to the embryonic jurist or theologian than the long sermons to which he was expected to listen.[224] At Bologna junior doctors and masters of medicine and arts might hold disputations once a week on holiday mornings, if a festival occurred within that period; otherwise the useful Thursday that served as a substitute was allotted to them for this purpose.[225] Doctors of law, however, might dispute during Holy Week, which fell within the Lenten period when they were supposed to maintain a thesis against all comers.[226] At some universities,

219 Angelus Carletus, fol. 128 r, § 30; Baptista de Salis, 217 v, col. 1, § 10.

220 *Cod. diplom. . . . di Pavia*, II, 469, 484, 497, 518, 537.

221 A. Fabroni, *Historia academiae Pisanae* (Pisa, 1791-95), I, 443-44, 445.

222 *Summa theol.*, pars III, tit. v, c. 2, § 5.

223 *Stat. . . . dello studio bolognese*, p. 108.

224 C. H. Haskins, " The University of Paris in the Sermons of the Thirteenth Century ", *Amer. Hist. Rev.*, X, 17. See also Seybolt, *Renaissance Student Life*, p. 33; l'Abbé Bourgain, *La chaire française au XIIᵉ siècle d'après les manuscrits* (Paris, 1879), p. 287; and Rashdall, *Univ. of Europe in the Middle Ages*, I, 479.

225 *Stat. . . . dello studio bolognese*, p. 260.

226 U. Dallari, *I rotuli dei lettori legisti e artisti dello studio bolognese del 1384 al 1789* (Bologna, 1888-1924), I, xxiii; see also Rashdall, *Univ. of Europe in the Middle Ages*, I, 219.

congregations were held on Sundays and feast days.[227] If the sermon of the morning had been an interesting one, delivered by an eminent theologian, a collation or informal discourse on the same theme might well claim the attention of a serious student of Paris.[228] On similar occasions, at Cahors, the residents of the College of Rodez had their wits sharpened by after-dinner disputations, the topic of which was posted in the hall on the previous evening.[229] Instead of a collation, the statutes of the College of St. Catherine at Toulouse stipulated that every week in which a holiday fell, a bachelor or a student of the college was to lecture on a decretal or to propose a question.[230] Thus it happened that, in devising ways to keep youths out of mischief,[231] colleges came gradually to assume some responsibility for the continuance of their academic work on holidays.

University authorities, however, were not entirely unaware of the loss to students which the frequent interruptions from saints' days caused. Statutes of Perpignan [232] and, at a later date, those of Vienna [233] show recognition of this fact. That the plurality of festivals was a disadvantage can scarcely be doubted when it is noted that, for the month of November, the *Ancient Kalendar of the University of Oxford* records eleven " non-legible " days exclusive of Sundays, which counted as holidays so far as university professors were concerned.[234] On simple feast days, cursory lectures on portions of the book reserved for extra readings seem to have been in order here, and some provision was apparently made for holidays on which reg-

---

227 *Fournier*, I, 414; III, 296-297, 298, 299; *Auctarium chart. univ. Paris.*, I, 435.

228 *Chart. univ. Paris.*, II, 692. According to M. Lecoy de la Marche, Jordan of Saxony introduced the *collatio* at the University of Paris to provide diversion for evenings, especially those of holidays, when students might be tempted to go abroad in search of adventure. See *La chaire française*, p. 463.

229 Fournier, II, 616.

230 *Ibid.*, I, 689; see also, *Cart. de Montpellier*, I, 621.

231 (Vienna) Kink, II, 196; (Perpignan) Fournier, II, 673.

232 Fournier, II, 673.   233 Kink, II, 390.

234 See pp. 100, 101.

ular lectures were suspended. The employment of a student's time, rather than the furtherance of his academic work probably lay behind the provision ' that, if, according to the calendar, it were a *dies non legibilis,* then the university authorities should arrange for a discourse on some book outside the regular curriculum *(de libro aliquo non usitato),* or should appoint a lecture on some section of a prescribed work which was usually reserved for " extraordinary " reading. In both cases, the material should, of course, be approved for holy days.' [235]

At the beginning of the thirteenth century, holiday lectures already embraced a large number of subjects. At Paris, in 1215, the course in arts, according to the definition of Robert de Courçon, included philosophy, rhetoric, the *quadrivialia,* the *Barbarisms* of Donatus, the *Nichomachean Ethics* of Aristotle and the fourth book of the *Topics* of Boethius, as approved material for feast-day reading.[236] With the passage of years, philosophy,[237] ethics,[238] and rhetoric [239] continued to be popular subjects for holiday lectures. Before the middle of the fifteenth century, Aristotle's works on metaphysics and natural philosophy, which had been banned in Robert de Courçon's day along with the heretical [240] doctrines of Amaury of Bène and David of Dinant, had received recognition and were looked upon as legitimate works for feast-day consideration.[241] By that time, at the University of Bologna, Greek literature, read either in the schools or at the home of the lecturer, was offered on such occa-

235 *Munim. acad.,* II, 371.   236 *Chart. univ. Paris.,* I, 78-79.

237 Dallari, I, 37, 40; *Cod. diplom. . . . di Pavia,* II, 433; Kink, II, 212.

238 Fournier, I, 426, § 22; III, 74, § 2; 166, § 15; 255, § 4. For the interest at Paris, see Rashdall, I, 444, n. 1; *Auctarium chart. univ. Paris.,* I, 199, 225; and G. Heidingsfelder, *Albert von Sachsen* (Münster in Westphalia, 1921), p. 55.

239 *Cod. diplom. . . . di Pavia,* II, 496; and Dallari, I, 19, 59, 62, 65, 70, 76. In the year 1395-96, the holiday lecturer in rhetoric was asked to read one of Dante's books (Dallari, IV, 18), but he may often have been allowed to choose his own material (Dallari, I, 74, 76).

240 *Chart. univ. Paris.,* I, 78-79.

241 *Cod. diplom. . . . di Pavia,* II, 309, 318, 356, 496, 520; Dallari, I, 27, 43, 73.

sions,[242] as were astronomy[243] and moral philosophy.[244] At Ferrara, the *Sophismata* of the Oxford scholar William of Hentisbery (fl. 1340), and a work on proportion by Albert of Saxony (d. 1390), followed by treatises *De instanti* and *De latitudinibus,* furnished material for holiday lectures in logic.[245] At German universities, which showed a growing tendency to provide lectures for feast-day afternoons, mathematics was sometimes introduced as a light subject well suited to such occasions.[246] By the fifteenth century, this sort of holiday lecture had attracted attention both at Bologna[247] and at Cambridge, where the statutes of foundations established during this and subsequent periods attest the success of its reception. According to the regulations of Queen's College, a discourse on mathematics was to be given in the hall on each feast day in the full term,[248] and at St. John's College, in the early part of the sixteenth century, it was stipulated that lectures in arithmetic, geometry, perspective, and the knowledge of cosmography and the sphere be arranged for holidays and vacations throughout the year.[249]

Inasmuch as the study of canon law on holy days had been stamped with ecclesiastical approval,[250] lectures on this subject were not only permissible, but popular also,[251] for at Bologna,

---

242 Dallari, I, 59, 81, 128, 137, 144, 157, 164, 176, 179, 185.

243 *Ibid.,* IV, 59, 63, 65.

244 *Ibid.,* I, 12-185, *passim; ibid.,* IV, 50, 63, 65. See also *Cod. diplom....di Pavia,* II, 230, 520, 528; and *Chart. univ. Paris.,* III, 452.

245 F. Borsetti, *Historia almi Ferrariae gymnasii* (Ferrara, 1735), I, 434-35. See also *ibid.,* I, 95, 96; *Cod. diplom....di Pavia,* II, 497, 520; and Dallari, I, 18, 21.

246 Kink, II, 196.   247 Dallari, I, 31.

248 Stat. of Queen's College, *Docs. rel. to Cambr. Univ.,* III, 51.

249 *Early Statutes of the College of St. John...the Evangelist in the University of Cambridge,* edited by J. E. B. Mayor (Cambridge, 1859), p. 385.

250 *Supra,* note 192.

251 Dallari, I, 10-186, *passim.* (See also *Cod. diplom. . . . di Pavia,* II, 166, 231, 279, 394, 537).

in 1444-1445, a third lecturer was added *vigore mandati*.[252] With increased interest in civil law, it too came to be read on feast days.[253] In some instances, we find the books under consideration enumerated,[254] and the time for the delivery of the lectures fixed as to morning or evening.[255] Reference has already been made to the fact that some authors of *Summae confessorum* questioned the legitimacy of professional study on holy days.[256] Whether this negative attitude represents an earlier point of view, or merely a prejudice gradually dispelled by the rising importance of medical studies, cannot now be determined. In any case, lectures in medicine as well as civil law were being given before the middle of the fifteenth century.[257] Avicenna's discussion of illnesses from head to feet [258] and Galen's work on crises [259] were favorite subjects, although surgery [269] and medical practice [261] were by no means neglected. If a professor were grounded in astrology as well as versed in medicine, the terms of his appointment to a chair in the medical faculty might include holiday lectures in prognostication as a part of his regular duties.[262] On one occasion, when such a

252 *Ibid.*, I, 19.

253 *Ibid.*, I, 9-187, *passim; Cod. diplom. . . . di Pavia*, II, 230, 236, 316, 355, 431, 495, 517, 538.

254 *Cod. diplom. . . . di Pavia*, II, 236. At Bologna, the books on which the lectures were given are usually specified; see, Dallari, I, 9, 10, 14, 16, 17, 30, 39, 42, 45, 49, 80, 92, 108, etc.

255 Dallari, I, 17, 22, 25, 28, 30, 33, 36, 95, 101, 103, 152, 177.

256 *Supra*, note 199.

257 Dallari, I, 11, 12, 15, 18, 23, 26; *Cod. diplom. . . . di Pavia*, II, 239, 281, 432, 470, 485, 539, etc.

258 Dallari, I, 107, 110, 112, 115, 118, 121, 124, 127, 130, 133, 137, 140, 147, 153, 160, 167, 173.

259 *Ibid.*, I, 73.

260 *Cod. diplom. . . . di Pavia*, II, 433.

261 Dallari, I, 99; *Cod. diplom. . . . di Pavia*, II, 222, 281. *Ad lecturam Practice Medicine*, the salary of Petrus de Monte Alcino, in 1418, was 781 flor. 8 s. (*Cod. diplom. . . . di Pavia*, II, 167) ; in the following year it was listed as 882 flor. (*ibid.*, II, 185).

262 *Cod. diplom. . . . di Pavia*, II, 413, 433. For other holiday lectures

stipulation was made at the insistence of students of Arts and Medicine, authorities of Pavia expressed the conviction that the university would derive profit from readings of this kind.[263]

Gautier de Chateau-Thierry's disapproval of Sunday lectures is proof that they were given in the thirteenth century.[264] The inclusion of *questiones dominicales* among the works of the canonist Bartolomeo of Brescia indicates that the practice of discussing topics on Sunday was not unusual before 1250.[265] By 1461, lectures in ethics were offered at Nantes on Sunday as well as on other holy days, and fees were levied for them.[266] At Angers, in 1494, Aristotle's *Ethics* was given at the hour of Prime, and his *Politics* was presented after dinner on Sundays.[267] The former lectures were supported by student fees, but payment for the latter was made by the Faculty of Arts.[268] At a later date (1526), the statutes of Cardinal College, Oxford, provided for *professores publicos,* who were expected, on Sundays and lesser feast days, to answer questions which had arisen in the minds of their auditors but which, from lack of time, could not be raised during the regular class period.[269] In the first chapter of his *Privilegia universitatum* Rebuffi reminds his readers that Christ taught on the Sabbath, a fact which leads him to defend the proposition that lectures may lawfully be delivered on Sundays.[270] Especially adapted to such occasions, he thought, were repeti-

in astrology, given under the Faculty of Medicine, see pp. 167, 272, 528. See also *Stat.... dello studio bolognese,* p. 259.

263 *Cod. diplom. . . . di Pavia,* II, 413.

264 See note 217.

265 Bartholomaeus Brixiensis, " Quaestiones dominicales antiquissimi iuris ... per titulos digestae," in *Quaestiones iuris variae ac selectae* (Lyons, 1572), pp. 89-138.

266 Fournier, III, 74, § 2.

267 *Ibid.,* I, 426, § 22.

268 *Idem.*

269 *Stats. of Cardinal College,* pp. 130-31.

270 Rebuffi, *op. cit.,* XVIII, fol. 33 r, col. 2, § 17.

tions,[271] which some students valued more highly than the lecture proper, because these were devoted to minute consideration of a point or a text already discussed.[272] Although Robert Goulet (fl. 1517), in his *Compendium,* suggested moderate relaxation for Sunday, he maintained that lectures ought to be given throughout the week, for, like the painter Apelles, he felt it a mistake to let any day pass without adding a line.[273]

271 *Idem.*

272 *Manuale scholarium,* p. 38.

273 R. Goulet, *Compendium,* translated by R. B. Burke (Philadelphia, 1928), p. 106.

CHAPTER III
PROTESTS AGAINST THE NON-OBSERVANCE OF HOLIDAYS

In the matter of Sunday and feast-day observance, theory and practice were often at variance. Responsibility for infractions of the law did not, however, fall wholly upon the laity, for the holiday conduct of both priest and prelate was included among the abuses in need of reform. On holy days when congregational duties ought to have rested heavily upon them because attendance at mass was then especially enjoined, clergymen seemed prone to abandon their charges and to wander abroad,[1] often on the pretext of preaching in an adjacent town [2] or paying visits to a neighboring shrine.[3] Some, without even making attempt at excuse, deserted their churches to engage in trade, and bartered and sold in scandalous fashion.[4] At matins and vespers a lamentable situation often prevailed. Then, conduct of the service frequently devolved upon a lone priest, or one accompanied by a single attendant. Owing to clerical interest in temporal affairs and amusements, it sometimes happened that the officiating minister was unable to celebrate the mass for lack of an assistant.[5] Carelessness in the performance of the offices on feast days,[6] neglect of holiday vestments,[7] and failure to come to choir at times of high festival [8] when music was an integral part of the service [9] were not unusual com-

1 Durandus, *op. cit., Tractatus illustrium . . . iurisconsultorum,* XIII, 181 v, rub. lii. See also 181 r, rub. 1.

2 *Dives and Pauper,* " Third command.", chap. 16.

3 The fulfillment of vows was sometimes undertaken for reasons not entirely religious. Clémanges, I, 145, col. 1.

4 *Visitations . . . of Southwell Minster,* pp. 22, 53. Such criticism had, of course, a wider application but was especially pertinent in the case of holiday behavior.

5 Clémanges, I, 143, col. 2.

6 *Fabric Rolls of York,* pp. 251-52; Peckham's *Registrum,* III, 981.

7 *Fabric Rolls of York,* p. 253.

8 *Visitations . . . of Southwell Minster,* pp. 49, 51.

9 *Fabric Rolls of York,* p. 243.

plaints. Such defections on the part of ecclesiastics, serious enough in themselves, were of double consequence when their effect upon the laity was considered. To advocates of the reform movement, it seemed unreasonable to expect congregations to hear services reverently, and in their entirety, when members of the clergy manifested great indifference toward the Church and its offices.[10]

The people's neglect of church attendance,[11] their casual interest in the service when they did go,[12] and their preoccupation with worldly affairs [13] furnished the topic of many a medieval discourse. Toward the beginning of our period Berthold von Regensburg, in one of his sermons, lamented the fact that, on holy days, pleasures were preferred to masses, and idle pursuits to the worship of God. Regardless of how brief a service might be, it always proved of too great length, he declared.[14] William Durand, the Younger, voiced the same complaint in his charge that Sundays and saints' days were not kept as the law bade, for people appeared to care only for songs, jests, dances, and unseemly chants—vanities with which they busied themselves within the church itself, and its precincts.[15] Disregard of holy days in the early fourteenth century troubled Guillaume le Maire of Angers, for he wrote:

10 Durandus, *op. cit.*, XIII, 181 v, rub. lii.

11 The number of episcopal ordinances pertaining to attendance is evidence of people's negligence. In extreme cases, offenders were summoned to the archdeacon's court. See *Depos. and Eccl. Proceed. of the Court of Durham,* pp. 27-28, 35; and Hale, *Preced. and Proceed. . . . from Eccl. Courts,* pp. 5, 83, 87.

12 Some scarcely remained long enough to say a *Pater noster,* complains Durandus (*loc. cit.,* rub. lii).

13 In a letter to the papal nuncio, Peter Schott, defending Johann Geiler's criticism of long-standing abuses at Strassburg, tells how the bürgermeister held audiences, buying and selling went on at the church porch, and animals and articles being offered for sale were often carried through the church during the service. See Coulton's *Life in the Middle Ages,* I, 242.

14 *op. cit.,* I, 268. For other complaints about the length of the sermon, see Hauréau, " Guyard de Laon ", *Journal des savants,* June, 1893, p. 372.

15 *Tractatus, loc. cit.,* rub. liii.

In many districts of the kingdom of France there has grown up an irreligious custom, nay rather an abominable abuse, namely that on Sundays and the other important festivals of the year, dedicated to the Majesty of the Most High, when Christian people should cease from servile work, come to church, spend their time in divine service, and receive the food of the Word of God, which they sorely need, from prelates and other authorized preachers—at such times they hold markets and fairs, pleas and assizes. The result is that the faithful, savoring more of the flesh than of the spirit, desert the church and its services and congregate in such places, where they carry on their trade and their lawsuits. Whence it comes to pass that on those holy days on which God ought to be worshipped above all, the devil is worshipped; churches remain empty; lawcourts, taverns, and workshops ring with quarrels, tumults, and blasphemies; perjuries and crimes of almost every kind are perpetrated there. Hence it follows that the law of God, the articles of faith, and other things pertaining to Christian religion and the salvation of souls are almost entirely ignored by the faithful. God is blasphemed, the devil is revered, souls perish, the catholic faith is wounded; it is therefore very necessary to apply a salutary remedy to such error and abuse.[16]

Fifteenth-century criticism of a similar, but less scathing, sort was expressed by the author of *Dives and Pauper,* who found the people of his day sadly lacking in devotion to God and the Church. On Sundays and feast days they failed to attend mass, or came with apparent reluctance. Often they arrived late and withdrew before the pronouncement of the benediction. Their inattention and indifference they excused on the ground of the excessive length of the service. Much more to their liking were Robinhood ballads and the entertainments of the tavern.[17]

Churchmen of essentially spiritual natures were greatly disturbed by the casual attitude of many parishioners toward prayers and devotions. In rural districts, especially, it was their complaint that, on Sundays and feast days, people gathered without the church, where they talked of mundane affairs.

16 *Livre de Guillaume le Maire,* p. 477.
17 See "First command.", chap. 51.

Some counted it sufficient to enter for a few minutes at the time of the elevation of the host; others were content to see it from outside, and felt their obligations thus fully discharged without having set foot across the church threshold.[18] On holy days of importance, it was very apparent that scores of people were drawn to the church by the most worldly of motives.[19] Those who came from love of pageantry and color,[20] pride of station,[21] or fondness for appearing in gala attire,[22] manifested little interest in the service. Many, therefore, regarded it enough to sprinkle their foreheads with holy water; others paid homage to the Virgin; a goodly number, however, merely saluted the image of some saint portrayed on the wall, and in this perfunctory fashion dismissed the matter of orisons entirely.[23]

When all due allowance is made for a standard pattern of criticism, the emphasis placed upon religious indifference in the later Middle Ages cannot but be impressive. It stands in strong contrast to Abbot Suger's description of the enthusiasm of the throngs who flocked to Saint-Denis on saints' days and, by their very number, forced him, in 1140, to undertake the rebuilding

18 Alvarus Pelagius, *De planctu ecclesiae*, lib. II, fol. 147 r. Antonino of Florence makes a similar complaint: "On holy days they (peasants) spend little time on divine service or the hearing of the whole mass, but in games, in taverns, or in contentions at the church doors". (*Summa*, pars III, tit. viii, c. 4, § 13). Bernardino of Siena gives an unpleasant picture of country-folk who linger in a neighboring inn until they hear the sacring bell; thereupon they rush to the church and, after the most perfunctory of devotions, return in haste to their cups (*Opera*, III, 265, col. 1).

19 For Guillaume Pépin's comments on the attitudes of church-goers, see Coulton's *Life in the Middle Ages*, I, 243-44.

20 Boccaccio tells us that he went to the Church of S. Lorenzo on Holy Saturday to see the people rather than to attend the service (*Decameron* [Hutton, ed.], I, xxxi; *cf. Filocolo* [Moutier ed.], I, 5-6). See also Alvarus Pelagius's criticism of students (*De planctu ecclesiae*, lib. II, fol. 140 v).

21 Barclay, *Ship of Fools*, I, 220 ff. See also Chaucer's description of the Wife of Bath, *Prologue to Canterbury Tales*, lines 451 ff.

22 Étienne de Bourbon, *Anec. hist.*, p. 237, and Clémanges, I, 144, col. 2. Sumptuary laws sometimes stipulated that officials attend the principal church services to see that the regulations regarding dress were being observed. *Corp. stat. ital.*, V, 328; XIII, 225.

23 Clémanges, I, 143, col. 1.

of the abbey church, in order to accommodate the crowds.[24] From numerous complaints about worldliness, irreverence, and lack of interest in holy days, it must not be thought that strict churchmen completely ignored the existence of conscientious parishioners who went to mass, repeated their paternosters, and obeyed the precepts of the Church in regard to holiday observance.[25] Ecclesiastics touched by the spirit of reform were, obviously enough, chiefly concerned with non-conformists; such inconspicuous, orthodox folk as Chaucer's Plowman [26] were therefore taken more or less for granted, and rarely given literary mention. Men of the Middle Ages, like those of every generation, were fond of drawing comparisons between their own times and the golden age of former periods. In this instance, however, the criticism seems not wholly unwarranted, for the change in values which these writers deplore appears to have existed. When, in recommending to London authorities the imposition of fines for holiday transgressions, Thomas Arundel, Archbishop of Canterbury (1396-1414), complained that his contemporaries held temporal punishments in greater dread than clerical penalties, and felt that things which touched the body or the purse were more to be feared than those which killed the soul,[27] he unwittingly announced the arrival of a new day. In the matter of holiday observance, this shift of interest did not pass unnoticed. Gautier de Coincy, for example, remarked that the Church's hold upon the peasant had lost its vigor, for, when any of them was excommunicated because of failure to keep feast days or to heed admonitions in this regard, he continued to plow and to harrow as if the ecclesiastical hand had not been lifted against him.[28] Such defiance some

24 *Ouvres complètes*, edited by A. Lecoy de la Marche (Paris, 1867), pp. 216-17.

25 Clémanges, I, 150, col. 2.

26 *Canterbury Tales, Prol.*, lines 533 ff.

27 Riley, *Mem. of London*, pp. 593-94.

28 "Du vilain qui à grant poine savoit la moitié de son Ave Maria", in *Les miracles de la Sainte Vierge*, edited by l'Abbé Poquet (Paris, 1857), p. 625, lines 354-59.

reformers interpreted as a serious defection on the part of the people, but others regarded it as unmistakable evidence that the Church had failed in its mission.

From moral and social points of view, the non-observance of holy days presented problems of very grave consequence. Inasmuch as the profitable use of leisure has always proved a difficult matter, it is not surprising that untutored folk who could not turn to letters should have spent their holidays in unwise and even objectionable fashion.[29] On Sundays and important feast days, when labor was forbidden, puritans complained that men stood idle in the streets,[30] or wasted their time and squandered their substance in play.[31] Sharper criticism of social conduct came from moralists who declared that holy days ought rightly to be called sorry days, since they were so largely dispensed in the devil's employ.[32]

Entertainment of the popular sort was to be found on public square and village green, where the beat of the dance and singers' voices mingled with the music of timbrel and zither.[33] Sometimes a roving jongleur recited a tale of romantic adventure,[34] or a group of actors presented a play.[35] On rare occasions neighborhoods even afforded the excitement of a tournament or joust.[36] Upon all vain amusements like these reformers looked with displeasure. Even such simple games as nine-pins and ball failed to meet with their approval, since harmless diversions were often accompanied by backbiting, slander, and scandalous

29 Clémanges, I, 148, col. 2-149, col. 1.

30 Alvarus Pelagius, lib. II, 147 r, § 16.

31 *Idem.;* see also Barclay *Ship of Fools,* II, 177.

32 Owst, *Preaching in Medieval England,* p. 180.

33 Clémanges, I, 145, col. 1.

34 People who complain about the length of the church services often enjoy listening half the day to accounts of jongleurs, says Guyard de Laon. (Hauréau. *op. cit.,* p. 372).

35 Many a medieval preacher laments the fact that people "rennen to interludes with great delijt". See Owst, *Preaching in Med. Eng.,* pp. 71, 81.

36 For references to tilts, tourneys, etc. on holidays, see Froissart, *Chronicles* (Bourchier's translation), V, 419 ff; *Reg. annal. coll. Merton.,* p. 185; *Decameron* (Hutton ed.), III, 136.

oaths [37] —evils exceptionally prevalent on holy days, according to all accounts.[38] Of the sins which flourished on such occasions, feasting and revelry were the commonest forms of offense. From early morning until far into the night the tavern was crowded. There men traded, placed their services, ate and drank to excess, and engaged in all manner of rude and boisterous fun. They sang lustily, played at tables and dice, challenged each other to feats of strength, and strove to outwit their companions with deceitful and fraudulent practices. Sometimes altercations arose; blows often followed; and, time out of number, revellers were haled into court for having taken part in a brawl.[39]

Disorderly conduct was by no means the only form of misdemeanor and crime which marked the holy day. On Sundays and feast days when infraction of the law was considered a double offense, occasion for raising the hue and cry was given again and again. While good Christian people were at church attending the mass, the impious saw fit to profit by their absence. Thieves looted houses;[40] apprentices wasted and purloined the property of their masters;[41] peasants pillaged their neighbors' orchards and vineyards, and took grain from their fields;[42] and divers laborers, servants, and grooms who kept dogs trespassed upon lords' parks and warrens, and damaged them with their hunting.[43] On special holidays like St. John's Day[44] and those of the Christmas season,[45] when a good deal of license was permitted,[46] some towns sought to insure peace

---

37 Barclay, *Ship of Fools,* II, 131.

38 Jacques de Vitry, *Exempla,* p. 233; *Handlyng Synne,* p. 287.

39 Clémanges, I, 144, col. 1.

40 Jacques de Vitry, *Exempla,* pp. 77-78.

41 Riley, *Mem. of London,* p. 218.

42 Jacques de Vitry, *Exempla,* pp. 77-78.

43 13 Richard II, st. 1, c. 13.   44 Riley, *Mem. of London,* p. 419.

45 *Ibid.,* p. 561.

46 At Lincoln, for example, an ordinance of 1480-1481 provided that, from St. Thomas's Day (Dec. 21) until the Feast of Epiphany (Jan. 6), "every denizen dwelling in the city was granted free liberte and saffegarde in

and order by increasing the watch and stipulating that vintners, tavern-keepers, bakers, and cooks were not to keep their doors open after ten of the clock.[47] As further safeguard to the public weal, streets and lanes were lighted by lanterns hung before houses,[48] and men were forbidden to walk about the town in defensive array.[49]

In university annals, unfortunate holiday incidents were not unknown, for bloodshed marked the famous Oxford town-and-gown affair on St. Scholastica's Day in 1353,[50] and at Paris, in 1367, injuries resulted from a quarrel between the guard and participants in a torch-light procession on the Feast of St. Nicholas.[51] Student transgressions, however, were ordinarily confined to such pranks as making off with the keys to the campanile so that the bells could not be rung, embarrassing lecturers by spiriting away their books, and blowing trumpets under windows of the schools so that professors were forced to dismiss their classes.[52] Such practical jokes were usually played at carnival-time when students donned costumes and danced with townsfolk in the streets.[53] Needless to say, academic authorities who felt that even visiting from house to house on festivals gave rise to " inconveniences ",[54] were wont to frown upon insolences like these.

While the state sought in no way to curb honest amusement, it saw that, under color of holiday festivities, a good deal of un-

honeste mirth and gam sportis to goo and doe what hym pleys ", and none was to be arrested for any " accion personelx " unless the king were a party. See A. Abram, *English Life and Manners in the Later Middle Ages* (London, 1913), p. 242.

47 Riley, *Mem. of London*, p. 581.   **48** *Ibid.,* pp. 561, 582.

49 *Ibid.,* p. 193; Smith, *English Gilds*, p. 427.

50 A. Wood, *The History and Antiquities of the University of Oxford,* edited by J. Gutch (Oxford, 1792-96), I, 456-461.

51 *Chart. univ. Paris.,* III, 166-175.

52 *Cart. . . . de Montpellier,* I, 382-383.

53 The three days preceding Lent were given over to merry-making, during which student excesses were not uncommon. See Seybolt, *Renaissance Student Life,* p. 68.

54 *Chart. univ Paris.,* IV, 643.

lawful agitation was fomented. In England, during the Scottish wars of Edward III,[55] in the time of Richard II [56] and that of Henry IV,[57] and during the reign of Henry V,[58] Christmas mumming called forth royal displeasure. Since it was feared that troublemakers in disguise might set afoot much mischief, men were forbidden, on pain of fine and imprisonment, to walk by night with feigned beards, painted visors, or deformed and colored visages, or thus to visit the houses of others, for the sake of playing at dice. A piece of legislation from the time of Richard II, prohibiting laborers and servants to keep hunting dogs and ferrets, illustrates even more clearly how discontent, lawlessness, and conspiracy—all concerns of the state—sometimes arose from idleness and flourished under cover of hunting and other such pastimes.[59] Merry-makings which accompanied the celebration of local church festivals were considered such advantageous places for furthering plans of insurrection that German authorities repeatedly sought to curtail the right of assembly during the years preceding the Peasants' Revolt.[60] On Sundays and other holidays, when the taverns were crowded, such leaders as Joss Fritz went quietly from group to group, spreading word of the movement, or mingled inconspicuously with the villagers in the churchyard or on the green, whispering news of the latest development in the plot.[61]

55 Riley, *Mem. of London*, p. 193; see also *Letter-book G*, pp. 274, 303.

56 *Letter-book H*, pp. 157, 293; see also Riley, *Mem. of London*, p. 534.

57 *Letter-book I*, p. 38. According to some chroniclers, the partisans of Richard II conspired, in 1400, to fall upon Henry IV under color of Christmas mumming. John Capgrave, *Chronicle of England*, edited by F. C. Hingeston-Randolph (London, 1858), p. 275.

58 Riley, *Mem. of London*, pp. 658, 669. On Twelfth-night, in 1415, Sir John Oldcastle and other Lollards were accused of attempting to cloak a seditious plot in similar fashion. See William Gregory's "Chronicle of London", in *Historical Collections of a Citizen of London*, edited by J. Gairdner (London, 1876), p. 108.

59 13 Richard II, st. 1, c. 13.

60 E. B. Bax, *German Society at the Close of the Middle Ages* (London, 1894), I, 36.

61 *Ibid.*, I, 63, 70, 89.

From the point of view of the state, sedition sometimes grew under the guise of piety itself. According to Froissart, John Ball spread his gospel of resistance to oppression on Sundays by preaching in the market-place to people returning from mass.[62] In a similar fashion, Hans Boheim, the Piper of Niklashausen, masked his socialistic designs under the cloak of religion. In the beginning, his Sunday and feast-day teaching consisted in exhorting peasants to abandon their present mode of life, to lay aside all personal adornment, and to make pilgrimages to Niklashausen, where homage to the Virgin was offered. From such a message, authorities had little to fear. The situation assumed another aspect when the prophet declared that he had received word from the Queen of Heaven to throw off all temporal and spiritual authority and abolish every form of oppression in order that universal equality might henceforth prevail. It goes without saying that such a doctrine readily gained supporters. Crowds flocked to Niklashausen, where the former piper was hailed as the new Messiah. Before the given Sunday on which this desirable state of affairs was to be realized, Hans Boheim was spirited away by order of the local bishop. In the struggle that ensued when his followers attempted to rescue him, some were killed and others taken prisoner. He himself was consigned to the flames, and so the movement ended.[63] How many uprisings of this sort were set on foot through holiday harangues cannot be determined, but it is safe to say that the enforced idleness of these days made men receptive to plans of this sort.

When failure to keep holy days rested on economic grounds, non-observance provoked especially sharp comment. Despite the Church's insistence that Sundays and important feast days be hallowed from vespers to vespers,[64] observance was often de-

---

62 *Chroniques*, X (Paris, 1897, edited by G. Raynaud), 96, 97.

63 K. Stolle, " Chronik ", edited by L. F. Hesse. *Bibliothek des literarischen Vereins im Stuttgart.* XXXII (Stuttgart, 1854). See also L. Fries, " Historia, Nahmen, Geschlecht, Wesen, Thaten ... der gewesenen Bischoffen zu Wirtzburg.... ," in J. P. Ludewig's *Geschicht-Schreiber von dem Bischoffthum Wirtzburg* (1713), pp. 852-55.

64 *Decret. Greg. IX*, lib. II, tit. ix, c. 1.

ferred until a much later hour.[65] In some occupations it was not always possible for workmen to leave their tasks at the ringing of nones or vespers. In the interests of the common safety, masons were obliged to close stairways and arches,[66] and for the sake of economy, founders were permitted to complete castings,[67] and furnace-tenders to maintain fires, if brick, glass, or lime operations had been under way for some time.[68] These conditions were, however, unusual, and did not affect barbers[69] and tailors,[70] who constantly offended by working until midnight on the eve of a holy day, in order that men might make a fine appearance on the morrow. Although moralists heaped reproaches upon the heads of these artisans, they were inclined to think that the frivolous trend of the times was also at fault in creating exceptional demand for such services then.[71]

To labor on the holy day itself stronger objection was made.[72] The practice of working at such times not only interfered with attendance at mass,[73] but sprang in large measure from covet-

---

65 In some districts the feast day was reckoned from midnight to midnight. Since this was not the usual practice, offenders could not be excused on these grounds, except in districts where the custom prevailed.

66 Boileau, *Les métiers et corporations . . . Paris*, p. 89, § 10.

67 *Ibid.*, pp. 53, § 5, and 54, § 9; and Riley, *Mem. of London*, p. 513.

68 Rodocanachi, *Les corp. ouvr. à Rome*, I, ciii.

69 Antoninus, *Summa,* pars III, tit. viii, c. 4, § 7; and Bernardino of Siena, *Opera*, II, 58, col. 1.

70 Antoninus, *Summa,* pars III, tit. viii, c. 4, § 4. Bernardino attributes the offenses of tailors to the fact that they often promise more work than can possibly be done, without violation of the holy day. (*Opera*, II, 58, col. 1.)

71 *Idem.*

72 Riley, *Mem. of London*, p. 593; *Little Red Book of Bristol*, edited by F. B. Bickley (London, 1900), II, 69 ff, 153. A protest from barbers themselves is implied in a pardon granted to a certain Robert Drayton of Coventry, who with others of the town conspired "that no barber should shave any stranger or workman or servant on feast days, thus making the cost of that art much dearer, to the damage of the whole people." A fellow-craftsman who would not be bound by these terms he maliciously harassed, and threatened with mutilation of his members. *Cal. of Patent Rolls,* 1391-96, p. 720; see also *Coventry Leet Book,* edited by M. D. Harris (London, 1907-13), p. xxxiv.

73 *Dives and Pauper,* " Third command.", chap. 8.

ousness and greed, churchmen believed.[74] Despite this conviction, and the Church's admonition that priests were accountable for the way in which holy days were celebrated in their parishes,[75] relatively few bishops appear, from their registers, to have carried on a very active crusade against holiday labor. One explanation for this failure may lie in the fact that, as moral offenses, these cases were often handled in the archdeacon's court, where transgressors were apt to receive severe treatment, according to some contemporary accounts.[76] Two entries from the journal of Eudes Rigaud of Rouen (d. 1275) show, however, that occasional prelates did not hesitate to deal summarily with those who offended in this regard. While riding from Meulan to Giset on a St. Matthew's Day, the Archbishop caught sight of men plowing. Since they had irreverently presumed to work on so holy a day, he caused their horses to be taken to Meulan, and would not allow the animals to be released until their owners had found bail, and promised to accept whatever punishment he should impose.[77] At another time Rigaud saw fit to place a heavy fine upon a carter's wife whom he discovered working with three horses on a Sunday.[78] A third instance of a churchman's attempt to enforce holiday observance is to be found in a letter which Thomas Arundel addressed, in 1413, to London officials, charging that the barbers of the city, being without reverence for God or His law, kept their houses and shops open on Sunday, and plied their trade as on other days of the week.[79] In response to his request that civil authorities strengthen his position by adding, to threats of excommunication, the penalty of fine, an ordinance was straightway enacted, forbidding any barber, or member of his household, to cut hair or shave within the city on Sunday, on pain of

74 Gerson, *Opera*, II, 560.   75 *Idem.*

76 Clémanges, I, 146, col. 1. Chaucer, however, implies that the possessor of a fat purse need have no fears of the archdeacon's court. (*Canterbury Tales*, Prologue, lines 653-662).

77 *Regestrum visitationum archiepiscopi Rothomagensis,* edited by T. Bonnin (Rouen, 1852), p. 375.

78 *Ibid.,* p. 501.   79 Riley, *Mem. of London,* pp. 593 ff.

paying 6s 8d for each offense.[80] That the town was a fairly effective disciplinary agent—and one not averse to enriching its coffers—may be surmised from the tenor of Archbishop Arundel's remonstrance; in conjunction with the gild, it probably did much to foster a healthy public opinion against infractions of the law. Sometimes town [81] and gild [82] officials even appointed inspectors to see that the statutes prohibiting holiday work were obeyed; in no place was their task more greatly facilitated than in Paris, where bakers were bidden by their gild to leave a lighted candle in their ovens, as evidence of good faith.[83]

Despite efforts to enforce holiday observance, a good deal of work seems to have been done on holy days in both towns and rural districts. The distinguished Franciscan Alvaro Pelayo, writing in the first half of the fourteenth century, found fault with peasants for plowing, harrowing, and transporting wood at such times.[84] Before the end of the century, John Bromyard (d. 1390) was also heard to complain that people of his day rarely gave up bodily labor on feast days. Either they gathered and stored the harvest, and did carting, or loaned their wagons to others. Although acts of charity are to be commended, the English friar was inclined to believe that, on holy days, such generosity did not deserve unstinted praise, for then service to God rather than to one's neighbor was due.[85] Country folk of the fifteenth century Antonino of Florence criticized for like reason; even on holy days he found that they brought beasts laden with corn and other things to their patrons, a practice which he strongly condemned, except in cases of dire necessity.[86] In cities and towns the situation does not seem to have

80 *Idem.*

81 A. Du Bourg, *Les corporations . . . de Toulouse,* p. 167; *Corpus stat. ital.,* VIII, 96-97. In this case, half the fine fell to the man who brought the accusation, half to the commune.

82 Rodocanachi, *Les corp. ouvr. . . . . à Rome,* I, cii.

83 Boileau, *Les métiers et corp. . . . de Paris,* p. 8, § 29.

84 *De planctu ecclesiae,* lib. II, fol. 147 r.

85 *Summa predicantium,* " Ferie ", § ix.

86 *Summa theologica,* pars III, tit. viii, c. 4, § 13.

been very different. From the number of occupations pursued, satirists were wont to declare that people postponed until the holy day much of the work of the week.[87] Finishing touches were put to garments,[88] carts rattled in the streets,[89] and elaborate preparations for feasting and good cheer were made by bakers, brewers, and cooks, who sought to enlarge their gains by taking advantage of holiday trade.[90] Disapproval of their conduct led the censorious to reflect with satisfaction that such folk would suffer in purgatory for disregard of holiday observance.[91]

Since the Church countenanced the purchase of bread, meat, and perishable victuals,[92] little criticism fell on other vendors of food, provided that they conducted their business during prescribed hours,[93] made their sales indoors,[94] did not neglect church services,[95] and devoted part of their profits to charitable causes.[96] It seems improbable, however, that shopkeepers always

87 S. Brant, *Narrenschiff,* p. 245.

88 In relating his experiences, Johann Butzbach tells how, as a tailor's apprentice, he was obliged to work until high mass on feast days of importance. *The Autobiography of Johannes Butzbach, a Wandering Scholar of the Fifteenth Century,* translated by R. F. Seybolt and P. Monroe (Ann Arbor, 1935), p. 93.

89 Brant, *op. cit.,* p. 246.

90 *Piers the Plowman,* C IV, 80-124; see also Bernardino of Siena, II, 56, col. 2.

91 *Piers the Plowman,* A VIII, 22.

92 *Decret. Greg. IX,* lib. II, tit. ix, c. 3; see also Wilkins, *Concilia,* III, 43, 74, 266. Sometimes the amount of purchase was limited by statute to small quantities. *Stat. di Bellano,* p. 110.

93 Sometimes shops were closed between nine and twelve. *Beverley Town Documents,* edited by A. F. Leach (London, 1900), pp. 124-25; *Coventry Leet Book,* p. 457.

94 This regulation applied to holiday sales in general.

95 It often happened that while good Christian men were attending the mass, regraters from their own, or neighboring villages, profited by their absence. See *Select Pleas of the Crown, A. D. 1200-1225,* edited by F. W. Maitland (London, 1888), I, 88-89.

96 Some gild statutes stipulate that part of the profit be set aside for the benefit of the confraternity. See statutes of the gold and silver smiths of Paris. Boileau, *Les métiers et corp....de Paris,* p. 33, § 8.

conformed to the regulations which governed holiday trade in their communities. In some places, for example, fruit dealers and green grocers were permitted to open their stalls, on condition that they made no displays;[97] butchers, to hang their meats, if they covered them;[98] and fishmongers, to stock their shops, if they had first attended the mass.[99] In Florence, chestnut-vendors were granted the privilege of selling their wares during the day, but might not roast chestnuts in public, although there seems to have been no objection to their doing so at home, behind closed doors.[100] In Paris, hawkers were allowed to cry their wines only once on Sundays, the eves of great feast days, and festivals of importance; on Good-Friday they were bidden to refrain from all selling, but might taste and appraise their wines after mass.[101]

In busy towns like London, sales of articles other than food appear also to have been lawful, provided that merchants acted with discretion. Cordwainers, for instance, were not permitted to display their goods in the market on Sundays, but they might serve people within their dwellings.[102] Haberdashers, too, were often governed by the same regulations,[103] or were allowed to open their shops in turn.[104] On Sundays and double feasts spurriers might indicate their business by hanging out a shop sign, but were obliged to conduct all selling under cover.[105] In some trades, sales were not countenanced on holy days, although merchants were granted the privilege of displaying their goods in the hope of attracting customers on the morrow. At Bologna [106]

97 Rodocanachi, *Corp. ouvr. à Rome*, I, xxxv.

98 *loc. cit.*   99 *loc. cit.*

100 L. Cantini, *Legislazione toscana* (Florence, 1800-1808), I, 372.

101 Boileau, *Les métiers et corp....de Paris*, p. 23, § 12.

102 At Bristol cordwainers might open their shops until seven o'clock. During the harvest season, they might serve the common people at any time, and travellers in need of shoes might always be accommodated. *Little Red Book of Bristol*, edited by F. B. Bickley (London, 1900), II, 168.

103 Riley, *Mem. of London,* p. 354.

104 Boileau, *Les métiers et corp....de Paris*, p. 114.

105 Riley, *op. cit.,* p. 227

106 *Stat. . . . dello studio bolognese,* pp. 20-21, rub. 19.

and Caen [107] books might be exhibited on Sundays and feast days, and at Toulouse dice-makers might show their stock to merchants interested in matching and comparing dice.[108]

The buying and selling at markets and fairs on Sundays and feast days was a more troublesome matter.[109] Sometimes the noise from the market-place was sufficient to detract from the solemnity of the church service,[110] for customers, and those who came for diversion, often engaged in such riotous fun that not infrequently quarrels and actual brawls resulted.[111] When, despite clerical denunciations and legislation to the contrary, the trafficking took place at the very church doors, it proved an even greater annoyance.[112] In England, by the later Middle Ages, the market proper had usually been driven from church-yard and cemetery,[113] but victualers and chapmen still went from town to town to sell their wares at the church on holi-days.[114] When asked his opinion regarding this practice, the author of *Dives and Pauper* condemned it without hesitation, on the ground that, at such times, no markets ought to be held either in or out of sanctuary.[115] With his dictum most church-men readily agreed. A few, like John of Freiburg and Angelo Carletti di Chivasso, however, felt that an occasional trip for the purchase of a forgotten necessity was permissible, provided that holiday markets were not forbidden in the district, and that one

107 Fournier, *Stat. . . . des univ. franç.*, III, 170, 213.

108 Sister Mary Ambrose Mulholland, *Early Gild Records of Toulouse* (in press) ; see " Statuta taxillorum," § 3.

109 In the early Middle Ages, the weekly congregation of people at church proved to be the most convenient time for the exchange of commodities,— especially of food stuffs, which formed the basis of most local markets. On theoretical and practical grounds, churchmen strongly opposed the general character of this buying and selling, and strove to abolish the abuses con-nected with it.

110 Wilkins, *Concilia*, III, 73-74.   111 *Ibid.*, III, 194.

112 *Leet Jurisdiction in the City of Norwich during the XIIIth and XIVth Centuries,* edited by William Hudson (London, 1892), pp. 17, 72. See also *Fabric Rolls of York,* pp. 248, 271.

113 Wilkins, *Concilia*, II, 295; III, 667.

114 *Fabric Rolls of York*, p. 271.   115 " Third command.", chap. 16.

did not make a habit of going.[116] Even these clergymen advocated foresight, and assured people that they would do much better to transact their business on the holiday eve.[117] This advice could not have been taken very seriously, for preachers continued to complain about the numbers who engaged in holiday buying and selling.[118] Owing to clerical insistence, some markets were, however, transferred from Sunday to other days of the week,[119] and correction was doubtless wrought in the conduct of those that remained. Lasting improvement was so difficult a matter to achieve that by the middle of the fifteenth century the English government felt called upon to assist in abolishing the scandals and abuses which had arisen in this connection. In forbidding the holding of markets and fairs on Sundays and such high festivals as Ascension Day, Corpus Christi, the Assumption of Our Lady, All Saints' Day, and Good-Friday, Henry VI was merely applying, in a larger way, regulations which bishops in England and on the Continent had laid down for their own dioceses.[120] By common consent, the opposition to Sunday markets was set aside during the harvest season, and some churchmen were inclined to think that the Sundays which fell within the period of fairs ought also to be exempted. Since periodic fairs were usually associated with saints' days, a good deal of traffic was inevitably carried on at such times. Undesirable as this situation proved, it was long before a complete change could be accomplished, because many laborers were free to leave their work on holy days only.

116 Johannes Friburgensis, *Summa,* lib. I, tit. xii, quaest. 12; see also Angelus Carletus de Clavasio, *Summa,* fol. 127 v, § 21.

117 Jacques de Vitry's opinion is given by Luchaire in his *Social France at the Time of Philip Augustus* (New York, 1929), p. 396.

118 Bromyard complained that there were few who, on holidays, did not go themselves, or send their servants with heavily laden beasts or carts, to the market. (*Summa pred.,* " Ferie "). See also Wilkins, *Concilia,* III, 68, 266, 365; Wykeham's *Register,* II, 416-17, 520-21; *Norwich Records,* II, 87.

119 In his article on market reform, Mr. Cate gives a long list of those which were transferred in England during the first half of the thirteenth century (*op. cit.,* pp. 55-65).

120 27 Henry VI, c. 5.

CHAPTER IV
OBJECTIONS RAISED TO THE OBSERVANCE OF HOLIDAYS

FROM conventional protests against the non-observance of Sundays and feast days apparently little was accomplished by way of reform, for complaints about the manner of holiday celebration show slight variation from century to century. To churchmen seriously interested in the correction of abuses, it therefore seemed that a more drastic view of the problem was needed. Against the institution itself was directed the criticism of these men who saw that, in losing sight of its high function, the Church had come to emphasize the form rather than the substance of its teaching. Indicative of the hollowness of such a practice was the popular impression that the keeping of holy days depended, in large measure, upon the meticulous observance of canons.[1] Of the real purpose or genuine significance of holidays little cognizance was taken. This changed point of view Erasmus illustrated in one of his colloquies [2] by telling how, despite the fact that loiterers and tavern-haunters created disturbances great enough to disrupt the church service and thus to defeat the purpose for which Sunday, the most solemn of holy days, was established, their boisterous behavior passed without comment. Yet had these same men but set a stitch in a shoe or eaten meat upon a Friday, they would have been dealt with severely. Such a state of affairs could only be counted a strange perversion of judgment.

Another aspect of this shift in values was manifest to Nicolas de Clémanges in the attitude of the Church toward holiday offenders. Indignant at its resort to practices which Christ

---

1 More, *Eng. Works*, II, 160-61. (The Messenger is puzzled by the attitude of farriers who regard St. Loy as their patron saint, yet, out of deference to him, prefer to let a horse mar its hoofs by running unshod rather than to shoe it on his feast day).

2 "'Ιχθυοφαγία," *Opera*, I, 803. Erasmus is a little unfair in his criticism, for we have already seen that preachers made complaint on this ground.

would have scorned, he made vigorous protest against the enforcement of holiday observance through vigilance of the archdeacon's court.[3] From what Chaucer tells us of this tribunal and its methods,[4] it is not surprising that Clémanges inveighed against the sending of summoners scurrying through the diocese to ferret out information concerning Sunday and feast-day violations. Upon detection of fault, culprits are said to have been haled into court and sentenced, less often in proportion to the weight of the transgression than at the discretion and will of the judge.[5] Although Clémanges entertained no thought of condoning holiday offenses or of advocating the non-enforcement of law, he nevertheless regarded the situation not unlike that in which Christ took the scribes and Pharisees to task for paying tithe of mint and cummin and omitting such essentials of the law as judgment, faith, and mercy.[6]

The tendency to create new feasts also exposed the Church to criticism. That multiplication lessened the value of holy days and fostered indifference toward them was not a novel idea, but one which gained ground slowly, owing, perhaps, to the report that the contempt of some heretical sects for ecclesiastical feasts was occasioned by the greatness of their number.[7] Among reformers who questioned the advantage of a multiplicity of festivals was Wyclif. If holy days engendered in human hearts a greater love for God and His law, then they were of profit, and it behooved men to keep them well; otherwise he considered them worse than useless.[8] Of like mind was Gerson, for, in a sermon delivered at the Council of Rheims in 1408, he deplored

3 Clémanges, *Opera*, I, 146, col. 1.

4 Prologue, lines 653-662; "The Freres Tale", IV, lines 1318, 1558.

5 Clémanges, I, 146, col. 1.

6 *Ibid.*, I, 146, col. 2.

7 Reinerius Sacchoni(?), "Contra Waldenses haereticos", edited by J. Gretzer, *Maxima bibliotheca veterum patrum et antiquorum scriptorum ecclesiasticorum*, XXV (Lyons, 1677), 265, col. 2. (For the incorrect attribution of this work to Reinerius Sacchoni, see the bibliographical note under his name.

8 *Select English Works*, edited by T. Arnold (Oxford, 1869), I, 330.

the accumulation of holidays, on the ground that they were often ill-observed and merely contributed to idleness and wrong-doing. To the problem in its entirety, he therefore urged prelates to attend, lest, by their number, festivals established in honor of God and for the good of the soul, become an affront to Him and a hindrance to salvation.[9] That it was the office of good churchmen to take counsel about these matters and to seek a remedy for them, Hugh Latimer pointed out to the Convention of the Clergy in 1536, on the eve of the English Reformation. In former periods, when holy days were fewer, they promoted goodness, honesty, and virtue; but, in his own time, he found districts so given to creating holidays without mean or measure that God was rendered a doubtful service thereby.[10] The change which holidays had undergone was also noted by Polydore Vergil, who questioned the result of their increase in number. Since he felt that the leisure which they afforded was devoted to the corruption of good custom rather than to worship and prayer, he was inclined to believe that holy days had outlived their usefulness.[11]

More critical expressions of opinion were provoked by specific proposals to add new feasts to the calendar. As early as the middle of the twelfth century, Potho, presbyter of Prüm (fl. 1152), had offered protest to the introduction of the Feasts of the Trinity and the Transfiguration. Not only did he consider the multiplication of holidays no indication of a people's wisdom and devotion, but he seriously questioned the advisibility of sponsoring a movement which the Church fathers had chosen to ignore. Why, he asked, should occasion be sought for offering to God a worship which is His due?[12] By arguments of this kind, expansion of the ecclesias-

9 *Opera,* II, 555.

10 H. Latimer, *Sermons,* edited by G. E. Corrie (Cambridge, 1844-1845), I, 52-53.

11 Polydorus Vergilius, *De rerum inventoribus* (Cologne, 1626), p. 433.

12 Potho, "De statu domus Dei", *Max. bibl. vet. script. eccl.,* XXI (Lyons, 1657), 502, col. 1.

tical calendar was by no means stayed. On the contrary, the movement increased so rapidly that, by the beginning of the fifteenth century, dioceses vied with each other in establishing new saints' days.[13] The grievous results of this practice Nicolas de Clémanges attempted to combat by setting forth its evils. Like Potho, he thought it deplorable for days which the Church fathers had purposely left free to be designated as the feasts of recently canonized saints.[14] Furthermore, prosperous periods, or ones of rejoicing after the passage of disaster, seemed more appropriate to the institution of new festivals than did times like his own, when the Church was torn by dissension and the realm mortally shaken by civil strife among its princes.[15]

From the ritualistic point of view, one of the chief objections to new feast days arose from the innovations necessary to their celebration. On this ground Pierre d'Ailly (1350-1420), in his treatise on the reformation of the Church at the time of the Council of Constance, opposed the solemnizing of so many new holidays.[16] Not only were new hymns and new prayers needed for such occasions, but writings bordering on the apocryphal were often read, while authorized Scripture was omitted.[17] The unwholesomeness of replacing old and established forms of service by new and untried ones Potho had also shown in his protest against additions to the calendar. The new offices for which these festivals called produced superficiality, and wrought changes in the service radical enough to have a profound effect upon monastic life, which he had been wont to regard as the bulwark of religion.[18] From ritualistic innovations brought about by the increase of holidays, Nicolas de Clémanges, too, believed that only confusion and instability could result.[19] Like

13 Clémanges, I, 157, col. 2.

14 *Ibid.*, I, 155, col. 2.

15 *Ibid.*, I, 154, col. 2.

16 "Tractatus de reformatione", H. von der Hardt, *Magnum oecumenicum Constantiense concilium*, I, 423.

17 *Idem.*

18 "De statu domus Dei", *loc. cit.*

19 Clémanges, I, 157, col. 2.

St. Dunstan,[20] he thought it a great mistake for a church to depart from the fixed order of its office, inasmuch as liturgical forms of long standing often served to distinguish one church from another.[21]

Since, for temporal advantage, churches were not averse to introducing new feasts [22] or to raising the status of ones already established,[23] alterations in the service sometimes arose from no special devotion to the saints, but rather from a desire to glorify a new foundation or a recently completed reliquary chapel.[24] When people were in straitened circumstances [25] and sufficient churches existed,[26] huge expenditures for the erection of elaborate and richly decorated structures seemed unjustifiable.[27] To

20 Dunstan forbade the churchmen of his day to discard any inherited liturgical uses which seemed to them fitting. D. Rock, *The Church of Our Fathers* (London, 1905), IV, 65.

21 Clémanges, I, 157, col. 2.

22 Relics enjoying popular favor were regarded as a great asset, since they enhanced the reputation of a foundation and greatly increased its revenues. When church or monastery was in need of repair, they were especially valuable. "At Salisbury, when the piers of the central tower began to cause anxiety, the Chapter advocated, and in 1456 achieved, the canonization of St. Osmund as a means of attracting pilgrims whose offerings at the shrine should be devoted to the repair of the fabric." R. L. Palmer, *English Monasteries in the Middle Ages* (London, 1930), pp. 101-02.

23 Desirous of having the church "made popular by suitable honors", the monks of the Monastery of St. Augustine, at Canterbury, petitioned Innocent VI to raise the status of the Feast of St. Augustine, Apostle to the English. W. Thorne's *Chronicle of Saint Augustine's Abbey, Canterbury*, translated by A. H. Davis (Oxford, 1934), pp. 560-61.

24 When St. Louis brought a piece of the Cross to Paris in 1241, a new holiday was established, on August 11, to perpetuate the memory of this translation, and that of the Crown of Thorns, which was enshrined in the recently-built chapel of Sainte Chapelle. Du Boulay, III, 170, 182; *Acta sanctorum*, see "August", V, 372 ff.; and Lecoy de la Marche, *La chaire française*, p. 371.

25 Objection to church-building at this time is made on the same grounds (*Dives and Pauper*, "First command.", chap. 51).

26 Clémanges thinks it more commendable to keep existing churches in repair than to build new ones (*Opera*, I, 158, col. 1).

27 Clémanges, I, 158, col. 1. Great churches with elaborate ornamentation often represent worldly pomp and civic pride rather than true devotion, says Dives. (*Dives and Pauper*, "First command", chap. 51).

such puritans as Wyclif, embellishments like stained glass, murals, and sculptured ornamentation, appeared a hindrance to worship.[28] When parishioners came to church on holy days, their curious interest in " gaye wyndownes, colours, peyntynges, and babwynrie " might easily distract them from contemplation of their sins, and turn their thoughts from heavenly things.[29] Inasmuch as the saints were especially inclined to act as intercessors on feast days,[30] it was essential that prayers and supplications then be offered with true devotion.[31]

Of holy days themselves, there was also much criticism, for these festivals were said to enhance the importance of the saints so greatly that their solemnities came in time to occupy a large part of the service. According to Clémanges, this state of affairs was not wholly of the people's choosing, for the majority seemed unwilling to have the saints venerated to such a degree that the worship of God was neglected.[32] When the deeds of the saints were recited at length, the reading of Old and New Testaments was greatly curtailed, or even omitted, perforce. By wholesome decree the fathers of the Church had stipulated that the Bible be used in the services of monastery, church, and convent. In former days, when the clergy had devoted themselves to the study of patristic literature and the instruction of the laity, with which they were charged, this regulation had been carefully observed.[33] Since Clémanges felt that nothing was more essential to the welfare of the Church than teaching com-

28 " Of the Leaven of Pharisees " ascribed to Wyclif, *English Works of Wyclif, Hitherto Unprinted,* edited by F. D. Matthew (London, 1880), p. 8.

29 *Idem.*

30 The victory at Agincourt was attributed by some of the English to the intercessions of the old Saxon saint, John of Beverley, on whose feast day the battle was fought. At the suggestion of Henry V, Bishop Chichele issued a constitution providing for fuller commemoration of this saint's festivals. (His deposition was celebrated on May 7, and his translation on October 25). Lyndwood, *Provinciale,* lib. II, tit. iii, c. 5.

31 Clémanges, I, 148, col. 1.

32 Clémanges, I, 156, col. 1.

33 Wyclif(?) complains that the friars of his day study law instead of holy writ. " Of the Leaven of Pharisees ", p. 6.

mon-folk to understand the Word of God, it was obvious to him
that faith would perish if the Bible were neither read nor
heard.[34] Through disuse and lack of devotion, a genuine distaste
for the Word was already to be found in some places. Although
it was granted that the lives of the saints produced wholesome
and even spiritual effects, their influence could not be compared
with the power derived from Holy Scripture, where the Spirit
itself speaks and imparts something of its vigor.[35]

Without doubt, the celebration of holy days and the consequent attention paid to the saints fostered superstition, and
furthered the materialistic character of the religion of the
Middle Ages. If credence is to be given to the accounts of contemporary authors, travellers prayed to St. Julian in the hope of
finding a good night's lodging;[36] housewives in search of lost
keys besought the help of St. Sith;[37] and usurers implored the
aid of the Virgin in placing their money at interest.[38] It was on
grounds such as these that Erasmus based his criticism of
church festivals. Although he wrote no treatise on holidays, his
ridicule of existing conditions proved an effective means of
combating the evils involved. He clearly saw how, in the course
of years, popular fancy had woven much of a legendary character about the lives of saints, and how superstitious beliefs and
practices often obscured the true purpose of holy days. While he
deplored the ignorance that prevailed, he understood and had
much sympathy for poor, deluded people. Like More, he did not
wonder if ' ruder minds were affected by the fictions of those
who thought that they had done a lasting service to Christ when
they had invented a fable about some saint.' [39] In his colloquy

34 Clémanges, I, 156, col. 2.

35 *Idem.*

36 Boccaccio, *Decameron,* II, 2.

37 More, *Eng. Works,* II, 160.

38 " Peregrinatio religionis ergo ", *Opera,* I, 775.

39 *Epistles,* translated by F. M. Nichols (London, 1904-13), I, 104. This
letter, formerly attributed to Erasmus, is now thought to have been written
by Thomas More to Dr. Thomas Ruthall, London, 1506.

The Rich Beggars, the great humanist shows how little was often known about a saint in districts where he was especially revered, and how ill-used was his festival by those who professed devotion to him. The Innkeeper has suggested that Conrad, a Franciscan, preach in the town on the morrow, which happens to be a holy day. Upon inquiry, the friar learns that the festival is that of St. Anthony, who is honored by the local populace because of his reputed guardianship of their swine, which thrive in the oak woods hard by. Knowing that the day will be marked by revelry and license, Conrad wonders that St. Anthony is not enraged with men who are more stupid than their own beasts. Only by imitating the saints in their lives does he feel that people show them true reverence.[40]

Especially open to criticism was the superstitious exaggeration of rites associated with some holy days—creeping to the Cross on Good-Friday,[41] singing the antiphony *Mentem sanctam* through the streets and squares on St. Agatha's Day,[42] and celebrating the Feast of the Purification with candle processions, for example.[43] That money spent, on such occasions, for tapers, church decorations, and the like, might be expended more wisely in charity was a sentiment which found expression in current opinion.[44] A conversation between two early sixteenth century students of Leipzig illustrates this point of view. Nicolaus, who is without funds, declares that he will not immediately become a heretic through failure to conform to the practice of carrying a lighted taper on Candlemas Day. If the pur-

40 " Franciscani ΠΤΩΧΟΠΛΟΥΣΙΟΙ ", *Opera,* I, 740-41.

41 This custom was strongly denounced in England at the time of the Reformation. Cf. S. R. Maitland, *Facts and Documents Illustrative of the History, Doctrine, and Rites of the Ancient Albigenses and Waldenses* (London, 1832), p. 530.

42 Lynn Thorndike, " Franciscus Florentinus or Paduanus, an Inquisitor of the Fifteenth Century . . .," *Mélanges Mandonnet,* II (Paris, 1930), 367. Franciscus Florentinus regrets that even learned men sometimes sanction such customs.

43 *Idem.*

44 See *Dives and Pauper,* "First command.", chap. 51.

chase price of candles were diverted to the poor, he believes that God would be far better pleased. For such a feeling his own impecunious state cannot be said to account entirely, because his friend, who is about to join the procession, agrees that, praiseworthy as is the aforesaid custom, it must neither take the place, nor lead to the neglect, of greater Christian obligations.[45]

Against holiday celebrations which were actually a travesty upon the church service, more vigorous protests were made. Of such a nature were the rites associated with the post-Nativity [46] feasts of St. Stephen, St. John, Holy Innocents, the Circumcision, or the Epiphany, when, through inversion of status, a portion of the service was in the hands of the lower clergy.[47] Inasmuch as the choristers, who presided on Childermas Day, were schoolboys and hence more amenable to discipline than were deacons, subdeacons, and priests, their conduct of the service under the Boy Bishop was more orderly, and hence met with relatively less criticism.[48] Although the mock election of the youthful prelate was sometimes decried [49] or even forbidden,[50] objectors to the custom often confined their complaints to the secular aspects of the celebration,[51] or were content to issue

45 Seybolt, *Renaissance Student Life*, pp. 65-66.

46 Sometimes the solemnity of the Christmas service was also marked by revelry. See von der Hardt, I, 733.

47 For a description of these rites, see G. Durand, *Rationale divinorum officiorum* (Lyons, 1612), lib. VI, cap. 15 (fol. 280 r and v) ; also fol. 522 v, for the account by Belethus.

48 In statutes where the festivities of Christmas week are considered as a whole, the ceremonies of the Boy Bishop receive as much condemnation as do those of the Feast of Fools.

49 In an injunction to Barking Nunnery, where this festivity was apparently popular, Peckham shows that he strongly disapproves of these rites and tolerates them only " cum displicentia ". See his *Registrum epistolarum,* edited by C. T. Martin (London, 1882-1885), I, 82.

50 *Infra*, Notes 61, 62. In 1423, the Parlement of Tours abolished the Feast of the Boy Bishop, when the choir-boys made a dog bishop. E. Giraudet, *Histoire de la ville de Tours* (Tours, 1873), I, 288.

51 Rigaud of Rouen forbade the nuns of the Priory of Villarceaux to indulge in their accustomed gaieties on the Feast of Holy Innocents. From what follows, it appears that they were in the habit of donning secular

ordinances limiting the ceremonies to the one day of the feast.[52] Unusual, however, may be counted decorum such as Conrad I (d. 918) witnessed at St. Gall, where the choristers' assumption of dignity greatly amused the royal visitor. When, with puckish humor, he sought to disconcert them by bidding his entourage roll apples down the aisle through which the boys were marching in procession, he found their youthful gravity unshaken by such untoward behavior.[53] From incidents of this sort it is obvious that the spectacle-loving people of the Middle Ages derived a good deal of entertainment from such ceremonials, and were not averse to injecting a riotous spirit into them on occasion. That the choir-boys themselves often indulged in hilarity is seen from chronicles [54] and casual entries like that from the *Fabric Rolls of York Minster,* which records the expense of repairing a large cross broken, by accident, on the Feast of Holy Innocents.

Under the subdeacons' conduct on Circumcision Day the service bore marks of greater revelry, for in their celebration, appropriately known as the Feast of Fools, were reflected many folk customs handed down from antiquity. Exceeding bounds, however, were the sacrilegious practices of wearing masks at the hours of office,[56] dancing in the choir in women's apparel,[57] running and leaping about the church,[58] and singing in dissonant fashion.[59] From an early date clerical behavior of this sort

clothes and dancing, either among themselves or with the people of the neighborhood (*Regestrum*, p. 44). Roger de Mortival of Salisbury complains because the children are "too much treated" at this time—probably on their visits to the houses of the neighboring gentry. F. A. Gasquet, *Parish Life in Medieval England* (London, 1906), p. 167.

52 Peckham, *Registrum,* I, 82-83.

53 Ekkehard IV, "Casus S. Galli", *Monumenta Germaniae historica* (Scriptores), edited by G. H. Pertz, II (1829), 84.

54 *Ibid.,* p. 91.

55 p. 74.

56 *Chart. univ. Paris.,* IV, 652-56.

57 *Idem.*

58 *Idem.*

59 Hampson, *op. cit.,* I, 146.

provoked remonstrances, especially in France, where the festival enjoyed its greatest popularity. The first of these protests was made in 1198, when, at the insistence of the papal legate, Eudes de Sully, Bishop of Paris, demanded that the shocking improprieties of the feast be abolished.[60] To the prelates of Gnesen in Poland, Innocent III, in 1207, issued similar instructions,[61] which were later incorporated into canon law under the *Decretals of Gregory IX.*[62] Before the publication of this general prohibition, the Council of Paris, held by Robert de Courçon in 1212, had directed both secular and regular clergy to refrain from celebration of the Feast of Fools,[63] and like steps had been taken by ecclesiastical assemblies at Avignon (1209)[64] and Rouen (1231).[65] These measures obviously met with indifferent success, for the injunction to abolish the festival, or to purge it of its abuses, appears at intervals in the disciplinary decrees of councils of the thirteenth,[66] fourteenth,[67] and fifteenth centuries.[68] To concerted attempts at reform churchmen lent individual support by seeking revision of the *Officium circumcisionis,*[69] or employing censure from the pulpit.[70] A few, like Odo of Tusculum (fl. 1245)[71] and Grosseteste of Lincoln (d. 1253),[72] took a firmer stand and strictly forbade the feast,

60 *Collection de documents inédits sur l'histoire de France.* Mélanges historiques, I (Paris, 1878), 73.

61 *Pat. lat.,* CCXV, 1070-1071.

62 *Decret. Greg. IX,* lib. III, tit. 1, c. xii (Friedberg, II, 452).

63 Mansi, XXII, 842, c. xvi.

64 Mansi, XXII, 791, c. xvii.

65 Mansi, XXIII, 216, c. xiv. For that at Rouen (1214), see *ibid.,* XXII, 920, c. xvi.

66 (Nevers, 1246), Mansi, XXIII, 731, c. iii; (Cognac, 1260), *ibid.,* XXIII, 1033, c. ii.

67 (Bayeux, 1300), Mansi, XXV, 66, c. xxxi.

68 (Paris, 1429), Mansi, XXVIII, 1098, c. ii.

69 It has been suggested that Pierre de Corbeil wrote the *Officium* with this purpose in mind (Chambers, *Med. Stage,* I, 281, 287-88).

70 Lecoy de la Marche, *La chaire française,* p. 368.

71 Mansi, XXIII, 683, c. iv.

72 *Epistolae,* pp. 119, 161.

on the grounds that it was scandalous and full of vanities odious to God but pleasing to the devil.

During the opening years of the fifteenth century, the attack upon the Feast of Fools was led by the theologian Jean Gerson, who condemned its celebration in sermon [73] and conclusions.[74] Because of the reluctance of cathedral chapters to suppress the festival, he found bishops unable to cope with the situation, and therefore believed that only by the intervention of royal authority could an end be put to the abuse.[75] No proposal involving state interference in ecclesiastical affairs could be expected to receive the endorsement of the clergy; yet strangely enough, in France a partial solution of the problem was achieved. For more than a quarter of a century after Gerson's crusade, the work of reform was carried on sporadically by provincial and diocesan synods.[76] More serious attention was given to the matter when the Council of Basel banned the Feast of Fools in its reformatory decrees of 1435.[77] Three years later, through promulgation of the Pragmatic Sanction of Bourges by Charles VII, this prohibition not only became ecclesiastical law but was likewise subject to execution by the *parlements* of France.[78] On account of the popularity of the feast, enforcement of the measure proved so slow and difficult that the Faculty of Theology at the University of Paris was moved, in 1445, to address to

73 In some dioceses, says Gerson, there prevails a great deal of superstition, of which the infamous customs associated with the feasts of Circumcision, Holy Innocents, Epiphany, and days preceding Lent are examples. By adapting sermons to the needs of their congregations, theologians might correct some of these common abuses, he feels. *Opera,* II, 109.

74 For the "Quinque conclusiones super ludo stultorum", see *Opera,* III, 309 f. Through the writing of letters, etc., Gerson says that he had for years labored to suppress these rites (*Opera,* IV, 620). For the letter sent from Bruges, in 1400, see *Opera,* I, 121.

75 Conclusion iii, *Opera,* III, 309.

76 For that of Tours, held at Nantes, 1431, see Giraudet, *op. cit.,* I, 289.

77 Mansi, XXIX, 108, c. xi. The Boy Bishop's celebration was also condemned.

78 *Ordonnances des rois de France de la troisième race,* XIII (Paris, 1782), 287-88.

the prelates of the country a letter of remonstrance, soliciting their aid in suppression of the evil. If the clergy persisted in celebrating the sacrilegious rites of the festival, it was proposed that offenders be treated as heretics and committed to the secular arm of the law.[79] Although this appeal, coupled with a rumor of the abrogation of the Pragmatic Sanction, led the king to enjoin stricter obedience to the law,[80] it was long before these ceremonies were abandoned, or passed, with other dramatic presentations, from the church to the street.[81] In England and other countries of western Europe, where its celebration met with less enthusiasm, the festival had a briefer history, and disappeared many years before it had ceased to be observed in France.[82]

As years passed, the material disadvantage of celebrating feast days in such numbers as to constitute virtually a second Sunday became increasingly apparent. Not only was the economic life of the period hampered by the frequent interruption of holidays, but the enforced idleness of these days lent itself to such license and disorder that further inconvenience resulted from men's unfitness for work on the morrow. To practical-minded reformers a long list of compulsory feasts seemed therefore singularly ill-suited to folk who lived by manual labor. Beyond the point of usefulness (in affording refreshment to body and soul), Gerson, for example, came to regard holy days as a great yoke laid upon people without their consent. Would that holidays were fewer, he exclaimed.[83] This sentiment was shared by Nicolas de Clémanges, who found the common folk of early fifteenth-century France so heavily burdened that he doubted whether, if released from holiday obligations and allowed to work on all days without penalty, they could hope

79 *Chart. univ. Paris.*, IV, 652 ff.

80 *Ibid.*, IV, 657.

81 See Young, *Drama of the Medieval Church*, Index.

82 *Idem.*

83 *Opera*, III, 1358.

to satisfy the demands made upon them.[84] In enjoining the observance of so many holy days the Church had obviously failed to take full account of the indigence of the populace, or their inability to put their leisure to profit.

Two illustrations will serve to show that the complaints of both artisan and rustic were largely economic. In 1524 the Silesian town of Breslau laid before the local bishop a formal protest against holy days.[85] The writ clearly showed that the townspeople were not opposed, in principle, to the veneration of the saints or the religious observance of their days. They counted it ill, however, that they were not permitted to follow their trades on feast days, many of which had been but recently established. Inasmuch as Silesia was a province in which the cult of the saints was carried to great lengths, their grievance was undoubtedly one of long standing,[86] and should not be attributed to the Lutheran movement, which was, by this time, well under way. The second complaint appeared in 1522-23, among the *Hundred Grievances of the German Nation*, presented to Charles V at the Diet of Nuremberg. This protest, however, did not pertain exclusively to Germany, or to the first quarter of the sixteenth century, but rather to a general situation that had existed in England and western Europe for a hundred years or more. According to this document, the people found themselves much oppressed by holy days, which had been created in such numbers that, despite their best efforts, farmers could scarcely find time to harvest and store the crops which they had forced with great labor from the ground. Since they saw that feast days no longer served a useful purpose, but were marked by transgressions too numerous and too patent to re-

84 *Opera,* I, 154, col. 1.

85 A. O. Meyer, *Studien zur Vorgeschichte der Reformation* (Munich, etc., 1903), p. 39.

86 The tenor of the accounts leads one to believe that other protests had preceded that of 1524.

quire proof, they declared this state of affairs a double annoyance.[87]

The husbandman's complaint against holy days was by no means new. In Roman times Cato,[88] Columella,[89] and other agriculturists [90] had looked upon religious festivals as a great inconvenience to be obviated in every possible way. So careful were they to make the most of the occupations which the pontiffs allowed on these occasions that Pliny agreed with the ancient oracles in counting him a poor farmer who performed on workdays labors which he might well have done on a festival.[91] For putting such a policy into practice, the Roman landholder with many slaves was more favorably situated than his medieval successor, who depended almost entirely upon the customary services of villeins. When canon law was strictly observed, the intervention of holy days worked to his disadvantage, for the time was commonly allotted to the villein.[92] The law of the

87 M. Goldast, *Collectio constitutionum imperialium* (Frankfurt, 1713), I, 466.

88 *De agri cultura* (Loeb ed., 1914), cap. 2, § 4 (p. 8). An overseer must sometimes be reminded that 'on feast days old ditches might have been cleaned, road work done, brambles cut, the garden spaded, a meadow cleared, faggots bundled, thorns rooted out, spelt ground, and general cleaning undertaken.' Cap. 138 (p. 120) shows that 'oxen might be yoked on feast days for the hauling of firewood, bean stalks, and grain to be stored.' Cato adds that 'for mules, horses, and donkeys, there are no holidays, except the family festivals.'

89 *De re rustica,* edited by J. M. Gesner (Mannheim, 1781), lib. II, cap. 22, " Quae per ferias liceat agricolae, et quae non liceat facere."

90 Virgil, *Georgica,* I, lines 268 ff ; see Loeb ed. of his works, I (London, 1920), 98, 100. 'Even on holy days, the laws of God and man permit the doing of certain tasks', says Virgil. 'No scruples ever forbade us to guide down the water rills, to protect a crop with a hedge, to set snares for birds, to burn brambles, or to plunge flocks into health-giving streams. Often too, the driver loads his donkey with oil or cheap fruits, and as he comes back from town, brings with him a millstone or a mass of black pitch.'

91 *Historiae naturalis libri XXXVII* (Paris, 1827-32), VI, 187 (lib. xviii, cap. 8).

92 *Historia et cartularium monasterii Sancti Petri Gloucestriae,* edited by W. H. Hart (London, 1863-1867), III, 116, 124, 158, 167, 190, 194, 200, 212.

Church, however, was frequently violated—a fact which shows more clearly than words how detrimental to lords of the demesne a multiplicity of holy days proved. In the interests of good administration, they therefore often resorted to an alternate arrangement whereby one feast fell to the lord, the next to the villein. Churchmen themselves were not averse to employing this system,[93] or to substituting another day's work for that lost through holiday observance.[94] Even on Sundays, which ought to have been free for rest and devotions, cartage,[95] court attendance,[96] or duties of a general character [97] were often required on the estates of business-like prelates. Despite the fact that peasants were in the habit of using at least a part of the holiday for such of their own work as local custom permitted,[98] extra services were often demanded of them then.[99] Although tradition may falsely ascribe the first outbreaks of the Peasants' Revolt to the Countess of Lupfin's insistence that tenants gather strawberries and snail shells on a given church holiday,[100] it is not difficult to understand how such trivial exactions might, through multiplication, have become a source of considerable annoyance.

In cities and towns it was those dependent upon daily wages who suffered most from holiday observance, for, as a usual

Cartularium monasterii de Rameseia, edited by W. H. Hart and P. A. Lyons (London, 1884-1893), I, 47, 288, 302, 311, 323, 399, 488, 492; *ibid.,* III, 284.

93 *Cart. . . . de Rameseia,* I, 350, 384, 398, 463, 492; *ibid.,* II, 22, 38.

94 *Ibid.,* I, 299, 302, 493.

95 *Ibid.,* I, 290, 300, 310; *ibid.,* III, 312.

96 *Court Rolls of the Manor of Hales (1270-1307),* edited by J. Amphlett and S. G. Hamilton (London, 1912), I, 121; *Select Pleas in Manorial and Other Seignorial Courts,* edited by F. W. Maitland (London, 1889), I, 7, 25, 38.

97 *Cart. . . . de Rameseia,* I, 290.

98 The attitude of the local clergy was often a determining factor. See Bennett, *Life on the English Manor,* p. 118.

99 On the manors of Ramsey, these services sometimes consisted of gathering nuts on St. John's Decollation Feast (Aug. 29), and collecting thorns for a wall at the Fair of St. Ives, on Maundy Thursday. *Cart.,* I, 290, 358.

100 Bax, *German Society at the Close of the Middle Ages,* p. 37.

thing, no payments were made for Sundays and feast days when work was forbidden.[101] To circumvent this inconvenience, masons, carpenters, plasterers, and other kinds of workmen resorted to the practice of engaging themselves for the week. Even when this arrangement resulted in a somewhat lower daily wage, holidays were apparently numerous enough to afford the men an advantage. In the hope of encouraging industrious habits and demonstrating the worth of the plan to employers, confraternities occasionally admonished their members to labor zealously on the work-day in order to be deserving of their holiday pay.[102] By the middle of the fourteenth century, however, London employers declared this practice so unprofitable that an ordinance forbidding its use was passed in redress of their grievance.[103] Although this prohibition was made effective throughout England by statutes of 1360 [104] and subsequent years,[105] the paying of wages for idle feast days was nevertheless continued, because of a shortage of labor.[106]

For practical reasons, it was not always possible to take note of the holiday in complex industries like building, where time and public safety were considerations of sufficient importance to justify the employment of feasts for advancing the fabric.[107] Although consecutive weeks of uninterrupted work were by no

101 *Munimenta gildhallae Londoniensis*, edited by H. T. Riley (London, 1859-1862) : " Liber custumarum ", I, 99; " Liber albus ", p. 728.

102 " A Poem on the Constitutions of Masonry " (probably written in the latter part of the fourteenth century) ; see J. O. Halliwell's *Early History of Freemasonry in England* (London, 1840), p. 20.

103 *Calendar of Letter-books . . . at the Guildhall of London,* edited by R. R. Sharpe (London, 1899-1912). *Letter-book F* (1350), p. 212.

104 34 Edward III, c. xi.

105 4 Henry IV, c. xiv (1402) ; 6 Henry VIII, c. iii (1514). See also, 6 Henry VI, c. iii (1427) and c. xii (1444-1445) ; *Little Red Book of Bristol,* I, 164.

106 *Cal. . . . Letterbook H,* p. 184 (1382).

107 Accounts of the building of the bell-tower at Merton College show a number of weeks of uninterrupted work, for a period of almost a year. See *Oxford City Documents, Financial and Judicial, 1268-1665,* selected and edited by J. E. T. Rogers (Oxford, 1891), pp. 314-322.

means typical,[108] the use of alternate feast days is frequently recorded in the expense accounts of great projects.[109] Master-masons, and others acting in a supervisory capacity, were often necessarily retained by the year,[110] and a clerk was assigned to holiday duty when loads of wood or stone were expected.[111] In industries other than building, where the disregard of feast days was less readily countenanced, the inconvenience of holy days must be estimated largely from clerical complaints, or instances of holiday work which came to the authorities' attention. The

108 At Avignon, in 1347, a fragmentary expense account for painters shows that, of the 107 days represented, fifteen were Sundays and eleven, feast days. Since no payments are recorded for these days, it seems reasonable to suppose that no work was done then. It should, however, be added that the scale of wages appears to be unusually high. See H. Denifle, " Ein Quaternus Rationum des Malers Matteo Gianotti von Viterbo in Avignon ", *Archiv für Literatur und Kirchengeschichte des Mittelalters*, IV (1888), 602-630. In the *Sacrist Rolls of Ely* (edited by F. R. Chapman, Cambridge, 1907) workmen's wages show deductions for holy days (Vol. II, p. 122, 123, 180). See also D. Knoop and G. P. Jones, *The Medieval Mason* (Manchester, 1933), pp. 118-121.

109 " Roll of Expenses for Works to the King's Palace at Westminster, 43 Henry III ", see *Issue Roll of the Exchequer, Henry III to Henry VI Inclusive*, translated and edited by F. Devon (London, 1837), pp. 43-74. See also " Fabric Roll of Westminster, 1253 ", in G. G. Scott's *Gleanings from Westminster Abbey* (Oxford and London, 1861), Appendix II.

At York Minster, during the restoration of the choir, the rules formulated (ca. 1352) for the masons and other workmen connected with the fabric show that, if two holy days occurred in one week, the men lost one; if three occurred, they were paid for half a week only. These regulations are especially useful, since they continued in force for about twenty years. See *Fabric Rolls of York Minster*, pp. 171-172.

110 See extracts from the account rolls of Edward III, pertaining to the work of St. Stephen's Chapel, as given in E. W. Brayley and J. Britton's *History of the Ancient Palace and the Late Houses of Parliament at Westminster* (London, 1836), p. 196; and D. Knoop and G. P. Jones, " The First Three Years of the Building of Vale Royal Abbey, 1278-1280 ", p. 15 (Reprint from *Ars Quatuor Coronatorum*, XLIV, 1931, pp. 5-47).

111 *Issue Roll,* 43 Henry III, p. 50. If the master-mason used feast days to adjust misunderstandings, etc., which had arisen in connection with the fabric, he was paid for his time, according to a statute of Avignon. See *Recueil de textes relatifs à l'histoire de l'architecture et à la condition des architectes en France, au moyen âge, XI-XII siècles,* edited by V. Mortet (Paris, 1911), p. 268.

value of these deductions is obviously limited, because the evidence applies only to the miller,[112] the farrier,[113] the fuller,[114] the tailor,[115] and the tanner [116] who did not escape detection. As long as the Church was content with condemning their sins of commission as marks of base avarice, it failed to recognize in such violation of the holy day one form of protest against holidays themselves.

Inasmuch as working days were largely devoted to the problem of making a living, it was inevitable—but contrary to canon law—that holy days should have been used for the conduct of miscellaneous affairs. In England, much of this business was allotted to Sunday, when the congregation of people at church afforded opportunity for the publication of proclamations,[117] the reading of charters,[118] and the procuring of witnesses for such transactions as the conveyance of land.[119] Sometimes wages [120] and fines [121] were paid, and not infrequently debts,[122] especially those due in installments,[123] were discharged on this day. Often gilds held their business meetings on Sunday,[124] and

112 Hale, *Extracts from Act-books of Eccl. Courts . . .*, p. 45, 164.

113 Mansi, XXVIII, 1108, c. 25.

114 *Depositions and Other Ecclesiastical Proceedings from the Courts of Durham . . .*, edited by J. Raine (London, 1845), p. 29.

115 *Ibid.*, p. 32.

116 Wilkins, *Concilia*, III, 218.

117 S. O. Addy, *Church and Manor* (London, 1913), pp. 201-202.

118 *Ibid.*, pp. 196-97.

119 *Northumberland and Durham Deeds*, edited by A. M. Oliver (Newcastle upon Tyne), 1929, pp. 17 (no. 56), 106 (no. 57), 113 (no. 94), 200 (no. 16).

120 Often bills for labor seem to have been paid on Sunday. (*Ledger-book of Vale Royal Abbey*, edited by J. Brownbill, Liverpool, 1914, pp. 195 ff). Bernardino of Siena condemns this custom of paying wages on Sunday because, through lack of funds, workmen are forced to postpone until the holy day their buying of necessary provisions. *Opera*, II, 58, col. 2.

121 *Cal. . . . Letter-book B*, p. 72.

122 *Ibid.*, pp. 83, 95, 97, 114, 119, 162.

123 *Ibid.*, pp. 65, 101, 127, 128.

124 J. T. Smith, *English Gilds* (London, 1870), pp. 10, 15, 23, 45, 62, 86, 94.

so, too, did some parishes [125] and towns.[126] Sunday assizes [127] and inquests [128] were by no means uncommon, and even the court of Westminster occasionally held session then.[129] On other holy days, similar conditions prevailed.[130] Local matters were settled,[131] rents so frequently paid that Martinmas and Lammas Day were retained, for convenience, in the post-Reformation calendar of the English church,[132] and routine business was continued, on a limited scale, in government departments like that of the Lower Exchequer, where administrative problems had greatly increased with the passage of years.[133] With better management, some of these activities might have been transferred to other days, but in many cases men were simply doing their best with an ill-fitting system.

125 *Ibid., The Parish* (London, 1857), p. 47.

126 *Beverley Town Documents,* edited by A. F. Leach (London, 1900), pp. 78-79.

127 *Three Early-Assize Rolls for the County of Northumberland, Saec. XIII,* edited by William Page (Durham, 1891), pp. xiii, 167.

128 *Court Rolls of the Manor of Hales,* II, 438; see also *Calendar of Inquisitions Miscellaneous* (London, 1916-37), II, 144 (no. 571), 146 (no. 578), 154 (no. 614), 155 (no. 618).

129 *Bracton's Notebook,* edited by F. W. Maitland (London, 1887), II, Cases 242, 248, 261.

130 For manorial courts held on feast days, see *Court Rolls of . . . Hales,* I, 183, 239, 253; II, 116, 163, 270, 366, 416, 538, 567. See also, for inquisitions, *Cal. of Inquisitions Miscellaneous,* II, 140 (no. 555), 141 (no. 558), 144 (no. 571), 146 (no. 578), 149 (no. 594), 153 (no. 608), 156 (no. 620), 160 (no. 644).

131 Mr. Thomas W. Simons finds that Englishmen of the late Middle Ages spent a good deal of their "leisure" time in the administration of local affairs. See the abstract of his unpublished dissertation, "Working Days, Holidays, and Vacations in England in the Fourteenth and Fifteenth Centuries", *University of Colorado Studies,* XXIV (1936), 65-66.

132 W. Gwynne, *The Christian Year* (London, 1915), pp. 92-93.

133 J. F. Willard, "The Observance of Holidays and Vacations by the Lower Exchequer, 1327-1336", *University of Colorado Studies,* XXII (June, 1935), pp. 281-87.

CHAPTER V

PRE-REFORMATION ATTEMPTS TO CORRECT HOLIDAY EVILS

DURING the three hundred years preceding the Reformation comparatively few of the men who protested against the multiplication of holidays and its consequent evils offered plans for reform. Most critics simply deplored the accumulation of feast days, lamented the use to which they had been put, and seemed content with calling attention to the need for stricter observance. Even Nicolas de Clémanges, who has left us the most important treatise on the subject, advocated, as a first measure, the correction of scandalous holiday behavior by the discipline of censure. Temperance, frugality, and industry, were the cornerstones upon which he proposed to build. If men saw the folly of wasting their earnings at tavern and market, he believed that they would apply themselves more zealously to useful labor. Thus he hoped to foster responsibility for home and family, and to supplant with wholesome interests the hazardous practices which flourished on feast days.[1]

Other churchmen, equally aware of the seriousness of the situation, but less concerned with material problems, sought to remedy conditions by emphasizing the spiritual significance of holy days. Among these was the mystic Thomas à Kempis (1380-1471), who counted as festivals only those which are celebrated in the heart. The sole reason for the frequent repetition of holidays he found in their being kept inwardly with great heartiness and joy, as a foretaste of everlasting happiness.[2] A similar point of view was expressed by Erasmus, who showed in his colloquy *The Religious Treat* that the observance of holy days, like certain religious obligations of the Hebrews, has ceremonial value, but is, in itself, of little worth. It assumes

1 *Opera omnia,* I, 148, col. 2.

2 *Opera omnia,* edited by M. J. Pohl (Freiburg im Breisgau, 1902-22), III, 77; IV, 193.

importance only as a manifestation of inner holiness, to which
it bears the relation of shadow to substance.[3] Such arguments
may have carried weight with a small group of lettered people,
but untutored folk could scarcely be expected to understand
metaphysical and abstruse conceptions of religion. While this
aspect of the subject was not to be neglected, it became increasingly plain that more concrete measures were needed, if much
was to be accomplished in the way of reform.

Now, in the course of generations, some churchmen who
realized how ill-spent was the holiday, had tried, in the interests
of decency, morality, and habits of industry, to bring about
a reduction in the number of saints' days. The first signs of this
movement were to be seen in local reforms. According to Robert
de Sorbon (1201-1274), his contemporary Guyard de Laon
abolished in his diocese of Cambrai many festivals which were
miskept there. In the diocesan calendar he is said to have retained the feast of only one martyr, St. Laurence, and that of
only one confessor, St. Martin.[4] From the vehemence with
which the good bishop speaks in one of his sermons of people's
reprehensible holiday behavior,[5] it is not surprising to find him
taking this step. Few prelates, however, were wise, courageous,
or even concerned enough to adopt a policy similar to that of
Guyard de Laon. He had, to be sure, an occasional follower,
for a century and a half later Nicolas de Clémanges [6] is found
bestowing high praise upon Michael [de Creney], Bishop of
Auxerre (d. 1409), for relaxing a large number of feasts observed in his diocese. The " detestable excesses " committed on
holy days led him to consider it more wholesome, and much

3 "Convivium religiosum", *Opera,* I, 679-80.

4 J. B. Hauréau, "Les propos de Maître Robert de Sorbon", *Mémoires
de l'Académie des inscriptions et belles-lettres,* XXXI, 135 f. According to
another account, Guyard de Laon, seeing that holy days were spent in dancing, tavern-haunting, and other questionable pursuits, gave his parishioners
permission to work on feast days of lesser importance. *Ibid.,* note to p. 136.

5 J. B. Hauréau, "Guyard de Laon, évêque de Cambrai", *Journal des
savants* (June, 1893), p. 372.

6 *Opera,* I, 151, col. 2.

more acceptable to God, to prune the vine and set out sprouts than to waste the day in tavern-haunting and indolence.[7]

The movement for the reduction of holidays was not confined entirely to local districts, however. As early as 1274, Humbert de Romans suggested to the Council of Lyons that men be compelled to keep no new feasts beyond those authorized by the Papal See.[8] In support of his proposal, he adduced the argument that holiday idleness contributed greatly to the increase of sin, and that laboring days were scarcely numerous enough to enable the poor to earn a living. As a partial solution to the problem, he advocated the granting of permission to work after mass on all but the major holy days of the Church.[9] Such a policy had already been begun, in a small way, at the Council of Oxford (1222), where, in a rather elaborate statement of observance, sanction for agricultural labor after mass was given on four feast days.[10] It was probably because of the labor shortage after the Black Death of 1348 that Simon Islip, Archbishop of Canterbury, in 1362, enjoined the clergy of his province to forbid the cessation of ordinary labor on feast days of lesser importance.[11] Although virtual abrogation of holidays through disregard was probably not a common occurrence, Bartolomeo Pisano's opinion that bishops, unsuccessful in opposing the introduction of festivals, might rightly allow them to pass without recognition,[12] indicates at least occasional resort to this method. Such an expedient, as Bartolomeo himself points out, would have been ineffectual in the case of holidays prescribed for the Church as a whole, but might have been satisfactorily used to reduce in number feast days of local significance.

7 *Idem.*

8 Mansi, XXIV, 130, c. 1.

9 *Idem.*

10 *Ibid.*, XXII, 1154, c. viii.

11 T. Walsingham, *Historia anglicana, 1272-1422,* edited by H. T. Riley (London, 1863-64), I, 297. The ordinance was obviously designed to check the shirking of work on minor feast days.

12 *Summa,* see "Feriae". Guyard de Laon probably followed a plan of this sort. See n. 4, *supra.*

During the fourteenth century the chief interest in holy days arose in connection with canonizations. As an exponent of the conciliar theory, Marsiglio of Padua (1270-1342) expressed the conviction that decisions concerning the canonization and veneration of the saints, the designation of holy days, and the consequent restriction of holiday labor should rest with a general church council.[13] In Marsiglio's opinion, the advantage of such a plan lay in its preventing a weak or base bishop from endeavoring to strengthen his position through public recognition of saintliness in the character of another.[14] There were, however, further recommendations for such a proposal: general agreement upon the qualities which entitled persons to canonization;[15] the focusing of attention upon great figures in church history rather than upon individuals who had attained sanctity through mere fasting and devotion;[16] fewer additions to the hierarchy of saints, owing to the removal of local interests;[17] and greater uniformity in church calendars.[18] To bishops

13 *Defensor pacis,* edited by C. W. Previté-Orton (Cambridge, 1928), p. 498.

14 *Ibid.,* p. 341. The editor suggests that it was the canonization of Thomas Aquinas by John XXII, in 1323, to which Marsiglio alludes.

15 According to the cardinals investigating the miracles of Edmund of Abingdon, in 1247, the rules of procedure were of such strictness that few of the early saints would have been canonized, had their lives been subjected to similar scrutiny. (Martène and Durand, *Thesaurus novus anecdotorum* . . . III, 1851). To people of heretical tendencies, the regulations seemed, however, to admit of a large degree of human error. Thomas More sought to ally the Messenger's fear that the Church might occasionally be misled in its choice of saints by assuring him that ' God would not suffer a mistake to be made in a matter so nearly touching His honor and worship '. T. More, *English Works*, II, 153.

16 For a student conversation on the relative merits of saints, see *Manuale scholarium,* p. 43.

17 John of Salisbury's life of Thomas à Becket, and that of Hugh of Lincoln by Giraldus Cambrensis, were both designed to pave the way for canonization, according to Mr. G. H. Gerould (*Saints' Legends,* p. 142). The pressure of local interests is better illustrated by the alacrity with which the names of three obscure Swedish ecclesiastics were presented for canonization after the cult of Bridget of Sweden had received formal recognition (von der Hardt, IV, 490, 707). Owing to the deposition of John XXIII, the re-

who strove to eliminate diocesan difficulties arising from variation in calendars, this last advantage would have been a great boon. With the expansion of commerce, it was inconvenient to find men idle in one parish and at work in another.[19] Before the turn of the century, the voice of Henry of Langenstein (1325-1397) was also raised in protest against further canonizations.[20] Is it fitting, he asked, that the names of Urban V,[21] Bridget of Sweden,[22] and Charles of Brittany[23] be added to the roster of saints when their number is already so large?

Like Protestant reformers of the Reformation, Wyclif[24] set little value on canonizations and saints' days, but considered Sunday of importance. His criticism was directed chiefly against the clergy, whom he found much more concerned about work

quest was carried to the Council of Constance, which appointed a commission to inquire into the lives and miracles of the reputed saints, and to see whether, in general, it would not be more fitting to diminish the number of saints rather than to increase it. In this connection, Jean Gerson, a member of the commissions, composed his treatise, *On the Trial of Spirits*. For the *De probatione spirituum*, see von der Hardt, III, pars iii, 28-38.

18 Emphasis on important feast days, and disregard of insignificant ones, was a method used to bring about greater uniformity in calendars. In his *Festial*, Mirk confines his attention almost entirely to the principal holidays of the liturgical year.

19 Mansi, XXIV, 812, c. xxiii.

20 His work " Consilium pacis; de unione ac reformatione ecclesiae in concilio universali quaerenda ", is published in von der Hardt, II, 1-60, and in Gerson's *Opera Omnia*, II, 810-840. For this reference, see von der Hardt, II, 56.

21 His canonization, promised as early as 1375, was delayed by the troublous character of the times; it was not finally accomplished until 1870.

22 Bridget was canonized by Boniface IX, in 1391. Owing to the insistence of the Swedish ambassadors, her canonization was confirmed by John XXIII, in 1415, and, after his deposition, by Martin V, in 1419 (von der Hardt, IV, 707, 708).

23 The process of canonization of Charles de Châtillon, Duke of Brittany, begun in 1369, was interrupted two years later and his veneration prohibited. His cult was not recognized until 1904, although his feast day had meanwhile been celebrated at Blois.

24 Wyclif was inclined, however, to make a distinction in favor of the earlier, rather than the later, saints (*Selected English Works*, III, 489).

done on insignificant feast days than about the desecration of the Lord's Day by sins of blasphemy, drunkenness, usury, and violence. Thoughtful men, he maintained, had no desire to burden common folk with additional holidays. In fact, they deplored the number which people were bidden to keep, for the observance of days seemed to them to partake of lust and greed rather than of charity and reason. If laboring people hallowed the Sunday well, he felt that they should be beset by no other " snares ".[25] Heretical sects adopted more radical views. The Hussites discarded the calendar of saints' days, but were inclined to refrain from work on Sundays.[26] Many Lollards, however, considered no day hallowed or holy, and put their conviction into practice by quietly working whenever they chose.[27] Inasmuch as the Waldensians found scriptural basis for the conventional idea of a sanctified Lord's Day, they observed Sunday, and the feasts of Christmas, Easter, Ascension Day, and Pentecost,[28] but rejected saints' days as inventions of the Church.[29] The more tolerant of the group thought it legitimate to follow the dictates of conscience, and saw no reason why members who wished should not honor the memory of the Virgin, the Apostles, and the Evangelists.[30]

25 *Ibid.*, III, 490-91.

26 Aeneas Sylvius, " Historia Bohemica ", in *Opera omnia* (Basel, 1571), p. 104.

27 *Fasciculi zizaniorum Magistri Johannis Wyclif cum tritico.* Ascribed to Thomas Netter of Walden; edited by W. W. Shirley (London, 1858), p. 428. See also Thomas Walsingham, *Historia anglicana*, I, 297.

28 Bernardus Guidonis, *Practica*, pp. 246, 248.

29 E. Comba, *History of the Waldensians in Italy,* translated by T. E. Comba (London, 1889), pp. 284, 323.

30 *Ibid.,* p. 311. See also, Bernardus Guidonis, *Practica,* p. 248; and the work " Contra Walden. haeret.", XXV, 265, col. 2, of *Max. bibl. veter. patrum,* etc. The more radical of the sect maintained, as did the Albigensians, that one day was like another, and therefore worked whenever they could without attracting attention. Although, as a group, the Albigensians had disappeared before the close of the fourteenth century, it is worth noting that they had been wont to celebrate several of the great Christian festivals for wholly unorthodox reasons. Christmas commemorated the descent of Christ into this wicked world; Easter, His triumph over its malignant ruler; and

Since holiday abuses yielded so slightly to correction, abrogation seemed to a few reformers the logical solution to the problem of saints' days.[31] Such a proposal Nicolas de Clémanges justified on the ground that ecclesiastical constitutions, though designed with laudable purpose, were not so inviolably binding but that they might be altered by the Church universal or particular, if circumstances demanded. By way of example, he bade his readers remember how, at one time, the Church universal had forbidden the use of images in its houses of worship, through fear that figures of wood and stone would prove a stumbling-block to converts. In later years, when these new Christians had become established in the faith, it had seen fit to abolish this statute by decree of general council. Sculpture and paintings were then made to serve the laity as books, in which even unlettered folk could read of Christ's life and ministry, and of the lives and struggles of the saints.[32] As a precedent for constitutional changes of a local character, Clémanges cited the aforesaid decision of Michael de Creney to delete holidays which had been instituted by his predecessors with good intent, but which later proved nothing but a detriment.[33] In order to forestall the critical comment that all things should be done for the benefit of the elect rather than for the sake of transgressors, Clémanges hastened to add the reminder that the Church never ceases to rejoice over the return of a sheep to the fold. In curtailing a number of miskept holidays, he felt that the Bishop of Auxerre in no way ignored those who were devoted to Holy Church and obeyed its commandments. They were still at liberty to hear divine service, and to render homage to the saints through prayer and meditation. Pious people who regretted the abolition of old solemnities doubtless took conso-

Pentecost, the establishment of the Catharist church. See C. Schmidt, *Hist....des Cathares ou Albigeois*, II, 137-38.

31 Clémanges, I, 145, col. 2-146, col. 2.

32 Clémanges, I, 151, col. 2.

33 *Ibid.*, I, 151, col. 1.

lation in the thought that this reform contributed to the welfare of their brethren.[34]

In the general program of reform, the problem of holidays received a modicum of attention at the Council of Constance. In his treatise on the reformation of the Church, written at the time (1416), Pierre d'Ailly suggested that saints be canonized less frequently, and that permission to work after mass be granted on all holy days except Sundays and the greater church festivals. The need for such measures was clearly shown, he felt, in the multiplication of sins on holidays, and in the difficulties of the poor in providing for themselves the barest necessities.[35] These are almost the identical words in which Humbert de Romans had presented his proposal to the Council of Lyons in 1274.[36] It is a sad commentary on attempts at reform that the intervening hundred and forty odd years had wrought so little improvement in conditions. If the anonymous treatise entitled *Capita agenda in concilio Constantiensi de reformatione ecclesiae* be correctly attributed to Francesco Zabarella (1360-1417), Cardinal-bishop of Florence, he too, strongly endorsed the movement for the reduction of holidays. In his opinion, feast days imposed a hardship upon poverty-stricken craftsmen and farmers, and were of no benefit to the state, since the leisure which they afforded merely served to lead the rising generation into mischief. He therefore proposed that only holy days enjoined by canon law be observed, and added that the general celebration of these holidays might well be confined to the principal diocesan church, and to the feast day of the church.[37] Inasmuch as Gerson, in sermon and tract, had already expressed his disapproval of the multiplication of saints' days,[38] he appears surprisingly inconsistent in seeking to advance the cult of St.

34 *Ibid.*, I, 151, col. 2.

35 von der Hardt, I, 423.

36 *Supra*, note 8.

37 von der Hardt, I, 513-14.

38 Mansi, XXVI, 1065; or Gerson, II, 555.

Joseph, which was then attracting attention.[39] On the Nativity of the Virgin, in 1416, he delivered to the Council of Constance a discourse in praise of Mary and Joseph, and proposed the institution of a festival in honor of the latter.[40] Since, at one point in his sermon, Gerson deplores the multiplication of holidays and seems averse to the introduction of new ones, it is possible that he thought of such a feast as enjoying a limited celebration among monastic orders rather than as being prescribed for the Church as a whole.

Although the Council of Constance adjourned without taking action in the matter, the efforts of Pierre d'Ailly and his associates were not entirely without results, for a paragraph pertaining to holidays was included among the recommendations presented to the Council by its committee on reform. This body granted that the number of saints' days had become excessive, and that useful employment was set aside to no purpose, since holidays were frequently spent in tavern-haunting, dancing, gambling, swearing, plundering, quarreling, and all manner of evil pursuits. It therefore proposed the abolition of festivals which had not been established by old laws, or by the decrees of church fathers. Especially advocated was the abrogation of less important holidays, and of those which fell during the summer season when the harvest and vintage must be garnered. As evidence that no disrespect to the saints was intended, the reformers suggested that deleted days be hallowed by the laity until the conclusion of the mass, after which they might pursue their occupations without ecclesiastical let or hindrance. The clergy, however, were bidden to solemnize these holidays at the regular canonical hours, and the feast of the patron saint of the

---

39 This increased interest is reflected in painting and sculpture; artists no longer portrayed Joseph as a meditative, or somnolent, figure. See *Revue de l'art chrétien*, XXXIII (1883), 370-71; and K. Künstle, *Ikonographie der Heiligen* (Freiburg, 1926-28), II, 353, 355. See also Otto Pfülf, " Die Verehrung des heiligen Joseph in der Geschichte ", *Stimmen aus Maria-Laach*, XXXVIII (1890), 156 ff., and 282 ff.

40 *Opera*, III, 1358. Several of Gerson's letters concerning the celebration of the Feast of St. Joseph are to be found in his *Opera*, IV, 729-36.

church was to be celebrated in each parish, according to custom.[41]

Interest in more immediate questions prevented the Council of Basel from considering the reduction of feast days, although its abolition of the Feast of Fools [42] is indicative of an attitude favorable to holiday reform.[43] Since this was the last of the great pre-Reformation councils, the subject of holiday reduction received scant attention during the remainder of the fifteenth and the beginning of the sixteenth centuries. Individuals, however, continued to puzzle over the problem, for some question of the propriety of disregarding holidays like Rogation Days and those of St. Anthony, St. Nicholas, and St. Catherine, which were celebrated from custom, is raised in the *Summae* of Angelo Carletti di Chivasso [44] and Baptista de Salis.[45] Their concurrent opinion that a person commits no mortal sin through the non-observance of feast days, unless failure to keep them is provocative of scandal, would have been considered almost heresy at an earlier period.

It was not until 1520, when Luther appealed to the Nobility of the German Nation for help in the work of reformation, that the matter of holidays again became an issue. As a practical measure, he then proposed the abrogation of all holy days except Sunday.[46] Although convinced that no one was obliged to hallow the Sunday, which seemed to him nothing but a ceremonial, Luther nevertheless realized that, like the Old Testament Sabbath, it was based upon two important principles—the need for periods of rest, and the allotment of time to God's service. Intelligent Christians would doubtless provide for

41 von der Hardt, I, 733-734.

42 *Supra*, chap. IV, note 77.

43 See Hemmerlin, " Tractatus de novorum officiorum divinorum institutione," *Variae oblectationis opuscula et tractatus*, fol. 49 v.

44 *Summa*, fol. 127 r, § vii.

45 *Summa*, fol. 216, col. 2, § ii.

46 "An den Christlichen Adel deutscher Nation von des Christlichen Standes Besserung ", § 18; see Luther's *Werke* (Weimar ed., 1883-1932), VI, 445.

both of these essentials; hence he saw no occasion for their keeping an appointed day, inasmuch as one day was no better than another. If they did not require rest on Sunday, they should not be censured for working then and taking their ease at some other time, he said. Rather different, however, was the situation of the common people, who bore much of the toil of the world. They needed regular days of rest, which also afforded them virtually their only opportunity to assemble for the hearing of God's Word. Inasmuch as Sunday had, from antiquity, been set aside for these purposes, Luther thought it wise to continue the practice.[47] If it seemed desirable to keep the festivals of Our Lady and those of the greater saints, he suggested that they be celebrated on Sunday, or at least in the morning with the mass, in order that the remainder of the day might be given to customary occupations.[48] By way of explanation, he wrote:

My reason is this; with our present abuses of drinking, gambling, idling, and all manner of sin, we vex God more on holy days than on others. And the matter is just reversed; we have made holy days unholy, and working days holy, and do no service but great dishonor to God and His saints with all our holy days. There are some foolish prelates that think they have done a good deed if they establish a festival to St. Ottilia or St. Barbara, and the like, each in his own blind fashion, whilst they would be doing a much better work to turn a saint's day into a working day, in honor of a saint.

Besides these spiritual evils, these saints' days inflict bodily injury on the common man in two ways: he loses a day's work and he spends more than usual, besides weakening his body and making himself unfit for labor, as we see every day, and yet no one tries to improve it.[49]

Within the next few years, however, two churchmen did what they could to alter conditions. In 1523, Bishop Cuthbert

47 *Werke,* XXX, Abt. 1, 143-147.

48 *Ibid.,* VI, 445.

49 *Ibid.,* VI, 446. The translation is that of H. Wace and C. A. Buchheim, *Luther's Primary Works* (London, 1896), p. 213.

Tunstall of London, after taking counsel with his associates, decreed that all churches of his diocese should adopt October third as their dedication day.[50] In this way, he hoped to eliminate the inconvenience resulting from the observance of this festival by individual churches at different times. In the following year, at the League of Ratisbon, the papal nuncio Cardinal Campeggio drew up, for the reform of the German clergy, a constitution in which the holidays to be observed were limited to those of general importance. Their number, however, was still far from small, for, in addition to Sundays, at least thirty-six feast days were to be retained. On lesser festivals, kept locally for one reason or another, men might, however, return to their work after hearing the mass.[51] At the Diet of Speier, in 1526, recognition of this ecclesiastical legislation, and of the protests of reformers, was taken in the proposal of a similar measure.[52]

The feeling that the observance of holidays had ceased to be purely a consideration of churchmen and moralists had been growing for a long time. As early as the reign of Richard II, the English crown had sought to turn the peasants' holiday leisure to good account by stipulating that servants and laborers practice archery on Sunday and other holy days, and refrain from " playing at tennis, quoits, dice, skittles, and other such importunate games ".[53] Under Edward IV, a similar ordinance provided for shooting at butts with the long bow upon all feast days. Since the Hundred Years' War made skill in the use of this weapon especially desirable, failure to conform to this regulation brought upon negligent or recalcitrant men a penalty for each offense.[54]

50 Wilkins, *Concilia*, III, 701.

51 Mansi, XXXII, 1088, c. xx.

52 J. Ney, "Analekten zur Geschichte des Reichstags zu Speier im Jahre 1526", *Zeitschrift für Kirchengeschichte*, IX, 153-54.

53 12 Richard II, c. 6.

54 17 Edward IV, c. 3. Five years later (1482-83), the excessive price of bows greatly diminished the amount of shooting, and " unlawful " games

In France, civil authorities appear to have been less successful in modifying or setting aside church legislation regarding holiday observance. A lawsuit between the town and the church of Saint Quentin will serve to show how such attempts were often looked upon as interference in a province strictly ecclesiastical. In 1442, the dean and chapter of the Church of Saint Quentin complained that the town listed in its statutes fewer holy days than the Church prescribed; that it unlawfully imposed fines upon shopkeepers who engaged in holiday trade; that it violated festivals which fell on Saturday by holding its market as usual; and that it exceeded bounds in granting, through an official, holiday permission to shoe a horse or render some other necessary service. When it was seen that these protests were being made to no purpose, the matter was taken to court. Since Saint Quentin was said to lie within the royal domain, the town was represented at the trial by one of the king's attorneys, who maintained that, inasmuch as the right of the king and his officials to regulate by statute the holiday work of barber, baker, and artisan had never before been questioned, he failed to understand why they should not issue ordinances affecting the holiday activities of merchants. For three reasons, the lawyer for the Church of Saint Quentin claimed that the position of the town could not be upheld. Only the Church, he contended, had authority to determine whether or not a feast was observed; the granting or withholding of permission to labor on holy days was included among its prerogatives; and to it belonged all fines levied for violation of holy days. After weighing the evidence, the court decided that the town had usurped the rights of the Church of Saint Quentin, and must relinquish all claim to the regulation of holidays. Since the civil authorities accepted their defeat, merchants were consequently forbidden to display or to sell their goods within the town on days of obligation.[55]

were again used (22 Edward IV, c. 4). This law was later confirmed by Henry VIII, in 1511-12 (3 Henry VIII, c. 3).

55 *Chart. univ. Paris.*, IV, 636-639.

In Germany, the political division of the country and the strength of the petty princes made it possible for a good deal of secular authority to be exercised in ecclesiastical affairs. The failure of the Roman Curia to carry out the recommendations of the Councils of Constance and Basel led the more pious of these German rulers to undertake, in their provinces, the work of reform. In his Constitution of 1446, William of Saxony, for example, insisted upon enforcement of the Sunday rest,[56] and, in a decree of 1457, Frederick of Brandenburg also enjoined stricter Sunday observance.[57] Since other princelings followed their example by frowning upon court sessions and similar infractions of the holy day,[58] considerable influence of a puritanical sort was exerted by the nobility. However, not all rulers who adopted a strong ecclesiastical policy felt bound to forbid holiday work or to enforce, in other ways, strict holiday observance. Albrecht of Prussia, for instance, is said to have pursued a middle course,[59] and Henry of Stolberg operated his mines on Sunday, with the consent of Sixtus IV, to whom he pointed out the fact that water would otherwise collect in his pits and endanger the lives of the miners.[60] Concern for the general welfare also led industrial towns like Breslau[61] and Mansfeld[62] to interfere in the matter of holiday observance. Since they saw how burdensome a multiplicity of saints' days proved, they sought to bring about a reduction in the number of church festivals, and to decrease the compulsory idleness which they entailed. In his *Address to the Nobility of the German Nation*,

56 J. H. Zedler, *Grosses ... Universal-Lexicon*, LV (1748), 1180.

57 *Codex diplomaticus Brandenburgensis continuatus*, edited by G. W. von Raumer (Berlin, 1831-1833), I, 239.

58 F. Priebatch, " Staat und Kirch in der Mark Brandenburg am Ende des Mittelalters ", *Zeitschrift für Kirchengeschichte*, XXI (1901), 79.

59 *Idem*.

60 *Regesta Stolbergica*, edited by Botho, Count of Stolberg-Wernigerode und Mülverstedt (Magdeburg, 1885), p. 615.

61 Meyer, *Studien zur Vorgeschichte der Reformation*, p. 38.

62 T. M. Lindsay, *History of the Reformation* (New York, 1906-1910), I, 141.

Luther undoubtedly expressed a current opinion in regard to the right of civil authorities to take such steps, when he wrote:[63]

One should not consider whether the Pope instituted these festivals, or whether we require his dispensation or permission to delete them. If anything is contrary to God's will and harmful to man in body and soul, not only has every community, council, or government authority to prevent and abolish such wrong without the knowledge or consent of Pope or bishop; but it is their duty, as they value their soul's salvation, to prevent it, even though Pope and bishop (that should be the first to do so) are unwilling to see it stopped.

Ideas of this sort were not confined to the Continent. In England they found expression in *A Dialogue Betwene a Knyght and a Clerke Concernynge the Power Spirituall and Temporall,* which John of Trevisa had translated from the Latin in the early part of the fifteenth century.[64] Immediately preceding the separation from Rome, they were also voiced in tracts like the *Supplicacyn for the Beggars* by Simon Fish, a

63 *Werke* (Weimar, 1883-1932), VI, 446; see also Wace, *op. cit.,* p. 214.

64 In reply to the Clerk's question as to whether a king could take from the Church privileges granted by his predecessors, the Knight answers:

". . . ye oughte to understande and knowe that what so ever the gouernours of the comon welth do, they intended it all together for the profite of the comon weale, hauynge regarde speciallye therunto accordynge to this rule. They dispose all thynges in suche wyse that they preferre the comon welthe before theyr owne; . . . Therfore it is knowen by witnes clere and true and eke by very reason, that they graunte nothyng by theyr writinge that shulde afterwarde be harme and domage to the common weale. But if any privilege that is graunted be founde and knowen hurtefull and greuous to the common weale, it maye be repelled and fordone in tyme of neede. Therefore it is not to be doubted, but that the hygh princeis for the necessary busynes of the realme, maye alter and chaunge (as reason and tyme requireth) the gracis and privileges to you granted, and by the lawes establyshed". See pp. 34-35 of the *Dialogus inter militem et clericum,* translated by John of Trevisa, and edited by A. J. Perry (London, 1925). The original, as *Disputatio super potestate praelatis ecclesiae, atque principibus terrarum commissa...sub forma dialogi inter militem et clericum,* is found in Goldast's *Monarchia sancti romani imperii* (Hannover, 1611-13), I, 13 ff. The treatise has been ascribed both to William of Ockham and to Pierre du Bois. For the question of authorship, see John of Trevisa, *op. cit.,* pp. xliii-xliv.

work belonging to the popular reformation literature of the period.[65] In 1532 appeared the so-called *Petition of Commons,*[66] which included, among its suggestions, a plea for the reduction of holy days,[67] especially of such as fell during the harvest season. Since the lack of devotion with which holidays were solemnized, and the abominable vices and wanton sports which flourished upon them were offered as occasion for the demand, there was nothing new either in the argument of the appeal, or its pious hope that such a measure would result in the remaining holidays being kept with more reverence. The implication that the king, by advice of his council, prelates, and ordinaries, could diminish the number of holy days, if he saw fit, was, however, alarming enough to bring a prompt reply from the bishops.[68] To the reformation of holy days they expressed a willingness to attend with all diligence, but showed themselves strongly opposed to any reduction in number. The festivals during the time of harvest were, after all, but few, they said—in August, the Feasts of St. Laurence, the Assumption of the Virgin, and St. Bartholomew; in September, the Nativity of the Virgin, the Exaltation of the Cross, and St. Matthew's Day, after which the harvest was commonly ended. Inasmuch as these feasts were of great antiquity, and served as special days of intercession, they felt that good Christian men would not be inclined to discard a single one. As a consequence of the bishops' stand, this petition received scant consideration, although it was one indication of the trend of the times.

A few years later, the interests of the state were well served by the publication of *A Treatise Concerning the Power of the Clergy and the Laws of the Realm,* in which the English law-

---

65 See p. 13, for a similar expression of opinion.

66 It was later established that the petition really emanated from the Court. See the introductory note to the *Petition*, H. Gee and W. J. Hardy, *Documents Illustrative of English Church History* (London, 1896), p. 145.

67 *Ibid.*, p. 150.

68 *Ibid.*, pp. 172-73.

yer Christopher Saint German (1460?-1540) set forth convenient political objections to holiday observance.[69] His discussion turns about the question of receiving into the Church an infidel king, who desires Christianity for himself and his people, but hesitates to bind his subjects to enforced idleness on holy days, and to the keeping of holidays other than Sunday. To his interlocutor, the author explains that, if, by divine law, the clergy have authority to institute holy days and to make decrees affecting both princes and their people, all Christians must obey their commands. If, however, holy days and ecclesiastical laws concerning them have been established by the clergy with the free consent of princes and people, or by grant of royal power, they may be set aside. Although Saint German believes that the Lord's example of resting from his labors on the seventh day imposes upon Christians the obligation to reserve one day of the week for prayer and contemplation, he sees no reason why the observance of this rest should not be transferred to some other day of the week, if, at any time, such a change appeared desirable. All holy days except Sunday, Saint German regards as mere ceremonials, developed through Christian devotion and the good example of priest and prelate. Because rulers have felt that their attention must be given to the weightiest affairs of the realm, they have delegated to the clergy certain matters pertaining to the good conduct of their subjects. This division of responsibility Saint German considers a serious mistake, for so important have ceremonials become that, for non-observance of them, transgressors suffer punishment more severe than that incurred for violation of divine law. Moreover, through advantageous use of their delegated power, the clergy have succeeded in causing the mandates of the Church to be held in greater awe than are the laws of the land. As a result of this extension of ecclesiastical authority, people are so grievously burdened that princes must now set themselves to the task of reform. If the multitude of holidays be found harmful to the commonwealth, and more conducive to vice than to

69 Published in 1535. Chapter X deals with the question of holidays.

virtue, Saint German insists upon the right of parliament to restrain their number. As a matter of expediency, however, he suggests the retention of feast days honoring Our Lady, the Apostles, and the greater saints. Regardless of whether these ideas represented infiltrations of Lutheranism, or developed independently on English soil from Lollard teaching, they must have been expressions of opinion extremely useful to the crown at the time of the English Reformation.

Soon after severance of its ties with Rome, the English Church defined its position in regard to festivals and saints' days. A decree of 1536, issued by Archbishop Cranmer, with the consent of Henry VIII and the clergy in convocation, stated that, as the number of holy days had become excessive. and, through men's superstitious devotion, seemed likely to increase, many of them had been abolished in the interests of the common weal.[70] The arguments supporting this decision were those which generations of reformers had used in protest against holiday observance: the undesirability of holidays on social grounds, their economic disadvantage, the misconception of their religious function, and their outgrown usefulness. In the future, each parish of the kingdom was bidden to commemorate the dedication of the church on the first Sunday in October; the feast of the patron saint, commonly known as the church holiday, was to be disregarded, unless, by chance, this anniversary coincided with a day observed for some other reason.[71] The decree also declared that, during the harvest season and term-time at Westminster, only feasts of the Virgin, the Apostles, St. George, and festivals on which the king's court did not sit, should be kept holy. In other words, men might lawfully work on all but a comparatively small number of specified days. There was, however, no objection to priests saying the

70 Wilkins, *Concilia*, III, 823-24.

71 *Idem.* In a letter to Cromwell, Sept. 5, 1536, Dr. John Tregonwell writes that "people are marvellously pleased that the King has allowed the *festum loci* of every church to be kept holy, at Cromwell's intercession." *Letters and Papers, Foreign and Domestic, of the Reign of Henry VIII* (London, 1862-1910), XI, 166.

service for the abrogated holidays, provided that they did not do so solemnly, or ring as for high festivals, or command the same to be hallowed.[72]

Fearing that a measure effecting such radical changes would evoke opposition, Henry VIII instructed Thomas Cranmer to see that the statement concerning " holidays abrogated and abolished as neither canonical nor meet to be suffered in a commonwealth because of inconveniences " be rehearsed to the local clergy. He wished no mention of deleted holidays to be made in the parishes, lest the people murmur, or continue in their accustomed idleness on these days.[73] Silence, however, did not always prove an effectual means of warding off trouble, for, in the Beverley district, the omission of St. Wilfrid's Day from the Sunday announcements brought upon the priest of Watton protest from the congregation. Hearing that this holiday, along with a number of others, had been put down by authority of the king and clergy in convocation, parishioners, in high indignation, declared their intention of celebrating holy days in accordance with their usual custom.[74] People in some of the northern counties took a similar stand,[75] and a few even went so far as to say that they saw no reason for their keeping holidays as they were kept at Westminster Hall.[76] Within the court itself there were signs of dissension, for Cranmer, writing to Cromwell about the opposition in Kent, reminded him of the difficulty in persuading men to abandon the deleted holidays, if the king's own household set the realm an example in breaking his ordinances.[77] The reluctance with which old observances were discarded showed how closely, in the course of

72 Wilkins, *Concilia*, III, 824.

73 *Ibid.*, III, 824.

74 *Letters and Papers ... of Henry VIII*, XII, pt. 1, no. 201 (p. 89). These protests were a part of the movement popularly known as the " Pilgrimage of Grace."

75 *Ibid.*, XII, pt. 1, no. 687 (p. 304).

76 *Ibid.*, no. 786 (p. 342).

77 *Ibid.*, XII, pt. 2, no. 592 (pp. 219-20).

centuries, these customs and traditions had been woven into the warp and woof of life. Only with effort did poor laborers adjust themselves to the new order.[78] In 1539, the situation in his diocese led the Bishop of Exeter to complain that, on the abrogated holidays, some fishermen were unwilling to cast their nets; that some carters refused to carry hay and other necessities then; and that, out of respect to St. Loy, some farriers declined to set a horse's shoe on his day. Attributing this state of affairs to lack of spiritual instruction, he admonished the clergy to teach their parishioners the folly of such superstitions, and to warn them that punishment would be meted out for like offense in the future.[79]

In some districts Cranmer found that it was the lower clergy who incited men to rebellion.[80] Contrary to the king's injunctions, they persisted in keeping the abrogated holy days solemnly, with singing and the pealing of bells.[81] A few, boasting that " old fashions should still flourish ", continued to deck the church and to march in procession.[82] Since conservative churchmen of higher rank found themselves in too precarious a position to offer much critical comment, it is difficult to know how general was their disapproval of the reform. Many must have agreed with those bishops who said, in reply to the *Petition of Commons* in 1532, that, inasmuch as the best of things are subject to abuse, it seemed to them more sensible to amend, rather than abolish, a misused institution.[83] Thomas More was of this opinion, for, like Colet, Erasmus, and other Oxford reformers, he saw no reason for discarding a good thing because wicked

78 See John Marshall's letter to Cromwell, *Letters and Papers . . . of Henry VIII*, XIV, pt. 1, no. 295 (p. 116).

79 Wilkins, *Concilia*, III, 846. For Archbishop Lee's instructions to the clergy of the diocese of York (c. 1538), see *Visitation Articles and Injunctions of the Period of the Reformation (1536-1575)*, edited by W. H. Frere and W. M. Kennedy (London, 1910), II, 51.

80 *Letters and Papers . . . of Henry VIII*, XII, pt. 2, no. 592 (pp. 219-20).

81 *Ibid.*, XI, nos. 431, 432 (pp. 172-73).

82 *Ibid.*, XII, pt. 2, no. 505 (pp. 192-93) ; XI, no. 514 (p. 206).

83 *Supra*, note 66.

folk put it to bad use.[84] This point of view he illustrates in one
of his conversations with the Messenger by citing a number of
instances in which it would be obviously foolish to delete a festival on account of the objectionable practices that had come to
be associated with it. He asks, for example, whether, in countries where men were in the habit of hunting on Good-Friday
morning, it would be better to break the custom or to abolish
Good-Friday. Inasmuch as the solemnity of Whitsunday processions was marred in a few cathedrals by the ribald songs of
some who followed the Cross, he wonders whether Whitsunday
should be abandoned or this evil corrected. In like manner, he
raises the question whether, because the Christmas season
was sometimes made a time of license and disorder, it would be
wiser to take Christians to task for misdemeanor or to give up
the celebration of Christ's Nativity. Those of the clergy who
had entertained little sympathy toward the movement for holiday reduction were doubtless grateful to More for his defense
of this position. Others, less affected by the issue, may have
thought, as did Agrippa of Nettesheim about the disputed date
of Easter, that vain controversies had arisen over sacred days
and seasons.[85] Among men who had advocated the curtailment
of holidays, there must have been rejoicing at the accomplish-
ment of a needed reform. In non-Protestant countries a similar
step was not taken until 1642, when, under Urban VIII, holy
days of obligation were substantially reduced in number.

84 More, *Eng. Works,* II, 167.

85 *De incertitudine et vanitate omnium scientiarum et artium liber* (n. p.,
1562), p. 227.

BIBLIOGRAPHY

Acta sanctorum Bollandiana, January-November 10. 65 vols. Edition published at Paris, etc., 1863 ff.

Addy, Sidney O. Church and Manor: A Study in English Economic History. London, 1913.

Agrippa von Nettesheim, Heinrich Cornelius. De incertitudine et vanitate omnium scientiarum et artium liber. 1562.

d'Ailly, Pierre. "Tractatus de reformatione, seu canones reformandi ecclesiam", H. von der Hardt, *Magnum oecumenicum Constantiense concilium de universali ecclesiae reformatione*, vol. I, cols. 409-433, and J. Gerson, *Opera omnia*, vol. II, cols. 903-916.

Alexander of Hales. Summa theologiae. 4 vols. Nuremberg, 1481-82.

The Ancient Kalendar of the University of Oxford from Documents of the Fourteenth to the Seventeenth Century. Edited by Christopher Wordsworth. Oxford, 1904. Oxford Historical Society Publications, Vol. XLV.

Angelus Carletus de Clavasio. Summa angelica de casibus conscientiae. Venice, 1487.

Antoine, Paul Gabriel. "De sacris Christianorum ritibus." [Extracted from his *Theologia moralis universa*.] See J. P. Migne and V. S. Migne, *Theologiae cursus completus...*, Vol. XIX (1841), cols. 1035-1140.

Antoninus of Florence. Confessionale. Strassburg, 1490.

——, Summa theologica, 4 vols. Verona, 1740.

Arrowsmith, Richard S. The Prelude to the Reformation: A Study of English Church Life from the Age of Wycliffe to the Breach with Rome. London, 1923.

Astesanus de Asta. Summa de casibus conscientiae. Eichstadt, 1480.

Auctarium chartularii universitatis Parisiensis. Edited by H. Denifle, E. Chatelain, C. Samaran, and others. 4 vols. Paris, 1894-1938.

Audelay, John. "Poem on the Observance of Sunday", *An English Miscellany, presented to Dr. Furnivall in honor of his seventy-fifth birthday*. Oxford, 1901, pp. 397-407.

The Autobiography of Johannes Butzbach, a Wandering Scholar of the Fifteenth Century. Translated by R. F. Seybolt and P. Monroe. Ann Arbor, 1935.

Azo of Bologna. Summa aurea recens, pristinae suae fidei restituta, ac archetypo collata. Lyons, 1557.

Baldus de Ubaldis. Consilia. 5 vols. Venice, 1608-09.

Baptista de Salis [Trovamala, Baptista]. Summa rosella. Venice, 1495.

Barclay, Alexander. The Ship of Fools. Edited by T. H. Jamieson. 2 vols. Edinburgh and London, 1874.

Baring-Gould, Sabine. Lives of the Saints. 16 vols. Edinburgh, 1914.

Bartholomaeus Brixiensis. "Quaestiones dominicales antiquissimi iuris . . . per titulos digestae." *Quaestiones iuris variae ac selectae*. Lyons, 1572. pp. 89-138.

Bartholomaeus Granchi a Sancto Concordio, Pisanus. Summa pisani, cum supplemento Nicolai de Aupimo. Reutlingen, 1482.

Bartolus de Saxoferrato. "Commentaria", *Omnia quae extant opera,* vol. VII, Venice, 1590.

Bax, E. Belfort. German Society at the Close of the Middle Ages. London, 1894.

Belethus, Joannes. Rationale divinorum officiorum. Bound with the Rationale of G. Durandus, fols. 486 r-568 v.

Bennett, Henry S. Life on the English Manor: A Study of Peasant Conditions, 1150-1400. Cambridge, 1937.

Bensen, Heinrich W. Geschichte des Bauernkriegs in Ostfranken. Erlangen, 1840.

Bernard, Frédéric. Les fêtes célèbres de l'antiquité du moyen âge et des temps modernes. Paris, 1878.

Bernardino of Siena. Opera omnia. Edited by Joannes de la Haye. 5 vols. Venice, 1745.

Bernardus Guidonis. Practica inquisitionis heretice pravitatis. Edited by C. Douais. Paris, 1886.

Berthold von Regensburg. Vollständige Ausgabe seiner Predigten. Vol. I edited by Franz Pfeiffer, Vol. II by Joseph Strobl. Vienna, 1862-80.

Beverley Town Documents. Edited by Arthur F. Leach. London, 1900. Selden Society Publications, Vol. XIV.

Bilfinger, Gustav. Die mittelalterlichen Horen und die modernen Stunden: ein Beitrag zur Kulturgeschichte. Stuttgart, 1892.

Boas, Frederick S. University Drama in the Tudor Age. Oxford, 1914.

Boccaccio, Giovanni. The Decameron. Translated into English anno 1620, with an introduction by Edward Hutton. 4 vols. London, 1909.

Boileau, Étienne. Les métiers et corporations de... Paris, xiiie siècle: Le livre des métiers d'Étienne Boileau. Edited by René de Lespinasse and François Bonnardot. Paris, 1879.

Borsetti, Ferrante. Historia almi Ferrariae gymnasii. 2 vols. Ferrara, 1735.

Bourgain, l'Abbé. La chaire française au XIIe siècle d'après les manuscrits. Paris, 1879.

Boyce, Gray C. The English-German Nation in the University of Paris during the Middle Ages. Bruges, 1927.

Bracton's Notebook: A Collection of Cases Decided in the King's Courts during the Reign of Henry the Third. Edited by F. W. Maitland. 3 vols. London, 1887.

Brant, Sebastian. Narrenschiff. Edited by Karl Simrock. Berlin, 1872.

Brayley, Edward W. and Britton, John. The History of the Ancient Palace and Late Houses of Parliament at Westminster. . . . London, 1836.

Britt, Matthew. The Hymns of the Breviary and Missal. New York, 1922.

Bromyard, Johannes de. Summa predicantium. 2 parts. Probably Basel, 1487.

Calendar of Inquisitions Miscellaneous Preserved in the Public Record Office. 3 vols. London, 1916-37.

Calendar of Letter-books Preserved among the Archives of the Corporation at the Guildhall of London. Edited by R. R. Sharpe. London, 1899-1912. (Letter-books A to L cover the years 1275-1497).

Calendar of the Patent Rolls Preserved in the Public Record Office . . .
   Richard II, 1377-1399. 6 vols. London, 1895-1909.
Calvin, Jean. Institution de la religion chrestienne. Edited by Jacques Pan-
   nier. 3 vols. Paris, 1936-38.
——, Tracts relating to the Reformation. Translated by Henry Beveridge.
   3 vols. Edinburgh, 1844-1851.
Cambridge Gild Records. Edited by Mary Bateson. Cambridge, 1903.
Cantini, Lorenzo. Legislazione toscana. Vol. I. Florence, 1800.
Capgrave, John. Chronicle of England. Edited by F. C. Hingeston-Randolph.
   London, 1858. Rolls Series, Vol. I.
Cartulaire de l'Université de Montpellier (1181-1400). 2 vols. Montpellier,
   1890-1912.
Cartularium monasterii de Rameseia. Edited by William H. Hart and
   Ponsonby A. Lyons. 3 vols. London, 1884-1893. Rolls Series, Vol.
   LXXIX.
Cate, James L. "The Church and Market Reform in England during the
   Reign of Henry III", *Medieval and Historiographical Essays in honor
   of James Westfall Thompson,* edited by J. L. Cate and E. N. Anderson.
   Chicago, 1938. pp. 27-65.
Cato, Marcus Porcius. De agri cultura. Loeb edition. Cambridge, Mass., 1934.
Chambers, Edmund K. The Medieval Stage. 2 vols. Oxford, 1903.
Chartularium universitatis Parisiensis. Edited by H. Denifle and E. Chatelain.
   4 vols. Paris, 1889-97.
Chaucer, Geoffrey. Canterbury Tales. Edited by J. M. Manly. New York,
   1928.
Clémanges, Nicolas de. Opera omnia. Edited by J. M. Lydius. Leyden, 1613.
Codex diplomaticus Brandenburgensis continuatus. Edited by Georg W.
   von Raumer. 2 vols. Berlin, 1831-1833.
Codice diplomatico dell' Università di Pavia. Edited by Rodolfo Maiocchi.
   2 vols. Pavia, 1905-15.
Columella, Lucius Junius Moderatus. De re rustica. Edited by J. M. Gesner.
   2 vols. Mannheim, 1781.
Comba, Emilio. History of the Waldensians in Italy. Translated by T. E.
   Comba. London, 1889.
Concilia Magnae Britanniae et Hiberniae. Edited by David Wilkins. 4 vols.
   London, 1737.
Cooper, Charles H. Annals of Cambridge. 5 vols. Cambridge, 1842-1908.
Corpus iuris canonici. Edited by Emil A. von Friedberg. 2 vols. Leipzig,
   1879-81.
Corpus iuris civilis. Edited by P. Krüger, T. Mommsen, R. Schoell, and G.
   Kroll. Berlin, 1922. The Institutes of Justinian have been translated
   into English by J. B. Moyle, 5th edition, Oxford, 1913; the Digest is
   also available through C. H. Monro's translation. 2 vols. Cambridge,
   1904-1909.
Corpus statutorum italicorum. Edited by Pietro Sella and others. 16 vols.
   Rome, 1912-33.

Cotton, Paul. From Sabbath to Sunday: A Study in Early Christianity. New York, 1933.

Coulton, George G. Five Centuries of Religion. 3 vols. Cambridge, 1923-1936.

——, Life in the Middle Ages. 4 vols. New York, 1928-30.

——, The Medieval Village. Cambridge, 1925.

The Court Baron, Being Precedents for Use in Seignorial and Other Local Courts, together with Select Pleas from the Bishop of Ely's Court of Littleport. Edited by F. W. Maitland and W. P. Baildon. London, 1891. Selden Society Publications, Vol. IV.

Coventry Leet Book, Containing the Records of the City Court Leet or View of Frankpledge, 1420-1555. Edited by Mary D. Harris, London, 1907-13. Early English Text Society Publications, Vols. CXXXIV, CXXXV, CXXXVIII, CXLVI.

Cruce, Franciscus de. Tractatus de festis. Probably Milan, 1475?

Cunningham, William. The Growth of English Industry and Commerce. 3 vols. 5th edition. Cambridge, 1910-12.

Dallari, Umberto. I rotuli dei lettori legisti e artisti dello studio bolognese del 1384 al 1799. 4 vols. Bologna, 1888-1924.

Denifle, Heinrich. Die Entstehung der Universitäten des Mittelalters bis 1400. Vol. I. Berlin, 1885.

——, "Ein Quaternus rationum des Malers Matteo Gianotti von Viterbo in Avignon", *Archiv für Literatur- und Kirchengeschichte des Mittelalters*. Edited by P. H. Denifle and F. Ehrle. Freiburg im Breisgau, 1888. Vol. IV, pp. 602-630.

Denton, William. England in the Fifteenth Century. London, 1888.

Depositions and Other Ecclesiastical Proceedings from the Courts of Durham, extending from 1311 to the reign of Elizabeth. Edited by James Raine. London, 1845. Surtees Society Publications, Vol. XXI.

Dialogue of Dives and Pauper: Compendyouse treatyse . . . fructuously treatynge upon the X Commandementes. Wynken de Worde, 1496. (Often attributed to Henry Parker).

Dialogus inter militem et clericum. Translated by John of Trevisa; edited by A. J. Perry. London, 1925. Early English Text Society Publications, Vol. CLXVII.

Dietterle, Johannes. "Die Summae confessorum (sive de casibus conscientiae) von ihren Anfängen an bis zu Silvester Prierias." *Zeitschrift für Kirchengeschichte*, Vols. XXIV (1903), pp. 353-374, 520-548; XXV (1904), 248-272; XXVI (1905), 59-81, 350-362; XXVII (1906), 70-83, 166-188, 296-310, 431-442; XXVIII (1907), 401-431.

[Dit] des vingt-trois manières de vilains: pièce du XIIIe siècle, with a modern French translation by A. Jubinal. Paris, 1834.

Documents Relating to the University and Colleges of Cambridge. 3 vols. London, 1852.

Döllinger, Johann Joseph Ignaz von. Beiträge zur Sektengeschichte des Mittelalters. 2 vols. Munich, 1890.

Dowden, John. The Church Year and Kalendar. Cambridge, 1910.

Du Boulay, César E. Historia universitatis Parisiensis. 6 vols. Paris, 1665-1673.

Du Bourg, Antoine. Les corporations ouvrières de la ville de Toulouse du XIIIe au XVe siècle, *Mémoires de la Société archéologique du midi de la France*. Vol. XIII (Toulouse, 1883-1885), pp. 154-253.

Duchesne, Louis M. Les origines du culte chrétien; étude sur la liturgie latine avant Charlemagne. 2nd ed., Paris, 1898.

Durandus, Guillelmus (the Elder). Rationale divinorum officiorum. 2 vols. Lyons, 1612.

——, Speculum. 4 vols. Lyons, 1547.

Durandus, Guillelmus (the Younger). " Tractatus de modo generalis concilii celebrandi ", *Tractatus illustrium in utraque tum pontificii, tum caesarei iuris facultate iurisconsultorum*. Lyons, 1584. Vol. XIII, Pt. I, fols. 154 r-182 v.

The Earliest Norwegian Laws, being the Gulathing Law and the Frostathing Law. Translated from the Old Norwegian by Lawrence M. Larson. New York, 1935. Columbia University. Records of Civilization, Vol. XX.

Early Statutes of Christ's College, Cambridge. With the statutes of the prior foundation of God's House. Edited with introduction, translation, and notes, by H. Rackham. Cambridge, 1927.

Early Statutes of the College of St. John the Evangelist in the University of Cambridge. Edited by J. E. B. Mayor. Cambridge, 1859.

Eisentraut, Engelhard. Die Feier der Sonn- und Festtage seit dem letzten Jahrhundert des Mittelalters. Amorbach, 1914.

Ekkehard IV. " Casus S. Galli ", *Monumenta Germaniae historica*. Edited by G. H. Pertz. Vol. II, pp. 84 ff.

Epistolae obscurorum virorum. The Latin text with an English rendering . . . by Francis G. Stokes. London, 1909.

Erasmus, Desiderius. Opera. Edited by J. Clericus. 10 vols. Leyden, 1703-06.

——, Epistles, from his Earliest Letters to his Fifty-third Year. Translated by F. M. Nichols. 3 vols. London, 1904-1918.

——, Opus epistolarum. Edited by P. S. Allen. 8 vols. Oxford, 1906-34.

Étienne de Bourbon. Anecdotes historiques: légendes et apologues. Edited by A. Lecoy de la Marche, for the Société de l'histoire de France. Paris, 1877.

Euvrardus ordinis Vallis Scolarium. Summa de festis. A thirteenth-century Ms. of the Bibliothèque de l'Arsenal, Paris, No. 401, fols. 3-401 v. This pagination includes both " Theumata " (fols. 399 v ff) and " Distinctiones " (fol. 401 v) of the work. Only the last two parts of the treatise have been read.

Evans, Joan. Life in Medieval France. London, 1925.

" Fabric Roll of Rochester Castle." *Archaeologia Cantiana*. Transactions of the Kent Archaeological Society. Vol. II (1859), pp. 111-132.

Fabric Rolls of York Minster, with an appendix of illustrative documents. Edited by James Raine. Durham, 1859. Surtees Society Publications, Vol. XXXV.

Fabroni, Angelo. Historia academiae Pisanae. 3 vols. Pisa, 1791-95.

Fasciculi zizaniorum Magistri Johannis Wyclif cum tritico. Ascribed to Thomas Netter of Walden. Edited by W. W. Shirley. London, 1858. Rolls Series. Vol. V.

Fitzstephen, William. "Descriptio Londoniae", *Liber Custumarum*, Vol. I, pp. 1-15.

Fournier, Marcel. La faculté de décret de l'Université de Paris au XVe siècle. 3 vols. Paris, 1895-1913.

——, Les statuts et privilèges des universités françaises depuis leur fondation jusqu'en 1789. 4 vols. Paris, 1890-94.

Fowler, Thomas. The History of Corpus Christi College. Oxford, 1893. Oxford Historical Society Publications, Vol. XXV.

Fries, Lorenz. "Historie, Nahmen, Geschlecht, Wesen, Thaten gantz Leben und Sterben der gewesenen Bischoffen zu Wirtzburg und Hertzogen zu Francken", in J. P. von Ludewig's *Geschicht-Schreiber von dem Bischoffthum Wirtzburg*, Frankfurt, 1713, pp. 373-866.

Froissart, Jean. Chroniques. Edited by Simeon Luce and Gaston Raynaud. 11 vols. Paris, 1869-99. For an English translation, see that by John Bourchier, Lord Berners, of the years 1523-25; with an introduction by W. P. Ker. 6 vols. London, 1901-03.

Gairdner, James. Lollardy and the Reformation in England. 4 vols. London, 1908-13.

Gasquet, Francis A. The Eve of the Reformation. New York, 1900.

——, Parish Life in Medieval England. London, 1906.

Gautier de Coincy. Les miracles de la Sainte Vierge. Edited by l'Abbé Poquet. Paris, 1857.

Gee, Henry, and Hardy, William J. Documents Illustrative of English Church History. London, 1896.

Geiler, Johannes von Kaisersberg. Ausgewählte Schriften. Edited by Philipp de Lorenzi. Trier, 1881.

Gerould, Gordon H. Saints' Legends. Boston and New York, 1916.

Gerson, Jean. Opera omnia. 5 vols. Antwerp, 1706.

Giraudet, Eugène. Histoire de la ville de Tours. 2 vols. Tours, 1873.

Goldast, Melchior. Collectio constitutionum imperialium. 4 vols. Frankfurt, 1713.

——, Monarchia sancti romani imperii. 3 vols. Hannover, 1611-13.

Gordon, Hilmar. Die Sonn- und Feiertagsgesetzgebung nach schweizerischem Recht. Zurich, 1917.

Goulet, Robert. Compendium recenter editum de multiplici Parisiensis Universitatis magnificentia, dignitate, et excellenti eius fundatione, mirificoque suorum suppositorum, ac officiariorum et collegiorum nomine. 1517. Translated by Robert B. Burke. Philadelphia, 1928.

Gower, John. Works. Edited by G. C. Macauley. Oxford, 1899-1902.

Gregory, William. "Chronicle of London", *The Historical Collections of a Citizen of London*, edited by James Gairdner. London, 1876, pp. 55-239. Camden Society Publications, Vol. XVII.

Gretser, Jacobus. De festis christianorum. Ingolstad, 1612.

Grimm, Jacob. Deutsche Rechtsalterthümer. 2 vols. Leipzig, 1899.

——, Weisthümer. 7 vols. Göttingen, 1840-78.

Grosseteste, Robert. Epistolae. Edited by Henry R. Luard. London, 1861. Rolls Series, Vol. XXV.

Guillaume le Maire of Angers. Livre de Guillaume le Maire. Edited by M. Celestin Port. Paris, n. d. Also *Collection de documents inédits sur l'histoire de France*. Mélanges historiques, Vol. XI² (Paris, 1877), pp. 187-569.

Gwynne, Walker. The Christian Year: Its Purpose and Its History. London, 1915.

Hale, William H. A Series of Precedents and Proceedings in Criminal Causes, Extending from the Year 1475 to 1640; extracted from act-books of ecclesiastical courts in the diocese of London, illustrative of the discipline of the Church of England. London, 1847.

Hales, Manor of. Court Rolls of the Manor of Hales, 1270-1307. Edited for the Worcestershire Historical Society by John Amphlett and Sidney G. Hamilton. 2 vols. Oxford, 1912.

Halliwell, J. O. The Early History of Freemasonry in England. London, 1840.

Hamilton, Mary. Greek Saints and Their Festivals. Edinburgh and London, 1910.

Hampson, Robert T. Medii aevi kalendarium, or Dates, Charters, and Customs of the Middle Ages. 2 vols. London, 1841.

Hardt, Hermann von der. Magnum oecumenicum Constantiense consilium. 6 vols. Frankfurt, 1700.

Hasak, Vincenz. Der christliche Glaube der deutschen Volkes beim Schlusse des Mittelalters. Regensburg, 1868.

Haselmayer, L. A. "The *apparitor* and Chaucer's Summoner". *Speculum*, Vol. XII (1937), pp. 43-57.

Haskins, Charles H. Studies in Medieval Culture. Oxford, 1929.

Hauréau, J. B. "Guyard de Laon, évêque de Cambrai", *Journal des savants*, June, 1893, pp. 365-374.

——, "Les propos de Maître Robert de Sorbon", *Mémoires de l'Académie des inscriptions et belles-lettres*, Vol. XXXI, pp. 133-149.

Hautz, Johann F. Geschichte der Universität Heidelberg. 2 vols. Mannheim, 1862-1864.

Heidingsfelder, Georg. Albert von Sachsen: sein Lebensgang und sein Kommentar zur nikomaschischen Ethik des Aristoteles. Münster in Westphalia, 1921.

Hemmerlin, Felix. Varie oblectationis opuscula et tractatus. Strassburg, 1498.

Henricus de Gorichem. Tractatus de celebratione festorum. Esslingen, 1474?

Henricus de Langenstein de Hassia. Consilium pacis: de unione ac reformatione ecclesiae in concilio universali quaerenda. (Written at Paris, 1381 A. D.) See J. Gerson, *Opera omnia*, Vol. II, cols. 810-40; or, H. von der Hardt, *op. cit.*, Vol. II, cols. 1-60.

Henricus de Segusio (Hostiensis). Summa aurea. Venice, 1586.

Herolt, Johannes (called Discipulus). Miracles of the Blessed Virgin Mary. Translated, with a preface and notes by C. C. Swinton Bland, and an introduction by Eileen Power. London, 1928.

Hessey, James A. Sunday: Its Origin, History, and Present Obligation. London, 1860.

Heywood, William. The "Ensamples" of Fra Filippo: A Study of Medieval Siena. Siena, 1901.

Historia et cartularium monasterii Sancti Petri Gloucestriae. Edited by William H. Hart. 3 vols. London, 1863-1867. Rolls Series, Vol. XXXIII.

Holweck, Frederick G. A Biographical Dictionary of the Saints, with a general introduction on hagiology. St. Louis and London, 1924.

Hospinianus, Rodolphus. Festa christianorum; hoc est, de origine, progressu, ceremoniis et ritibus festorum dierum christianorum. Zurich, 1593.

Hutton, William H. The Influence of Christianity upon National Character Illustrated by the Lives and Legends of the English Saints. 2nd edition). London, 1908.

Issue Roll of the Exchequer, Henry III to Henry VI inclusive. Translated and edited by F. Devon. London, 1837.

Jacobus de Clusa (de Jueterbog). Sermones de sanctis. Blaubeuren, ca. 1475.

Jacques de Vitry. The *Exempla,* or Illustrative Stories from the *Sermones Vulgares* . . . Edited by Thomas F. Crane. London, published for the Folk-Lore Society, 1890.

Janssen, Johannes. Geschichte des deutschen Volkes seit dem Ausgang des Mittelalters. 8 vols. Freiburg im Breisgau and St. Louis, 1896-1904.

Johannes Andreae. Constitutiones cum apparatu Johannis Andree. Nuremberg, 1482.

——, Liber sextus decretalium . . . una cum apparatu Johannis Andree. Nuremberg, 1482.

Johannes Friburgensis. Summa confessorum. Augsburg, 1476. Lib. I, tit. XII, Quaest. i-xiii. "De feriis et ieiuniis."

John of Trevisa, see Dialogus inter militem et clericum.

Kellner, K. A. Heinrich. Heortology: A History of the Christian Festivals from Their Origin to the Present Day. Translated from the second German edition by a priest of the Diocese of Westminster. London, 1908.

Kidd, Beresford J. Documents Illustrative of the Continental Reformation. Oxford, 1911.

Kink, Rudolf. Geschichte der kaiserlichen Universität zu Wien. 2 vols. Vienna, 1854.

Knoop, Douglas and Jones, G. P. The Medieval Mason: An Economic History of English Stone Building in the Later Middle Ages and Early Modern Times. Manchester, 1933.

Articles on the history of operative masonry in *Ars Quatuor Coronatorum:* "The Building of Eton College, 1442-1460." Vol. XLVI (1933), pp. 70-114.

"Castle-building at Beaumaris and Caernarvon in the Early Fourteenth Century". Vol. XLV (1932), pp. 4-47.

"The First Three Years of the Building of Vale Royal Abbey, 1278-1280". Vol. XLIV (1931), pp. 5-47.

Knox, John. Works. Edited by David Laing. 6 vols. Edinburgh, 1864.

Künstle, Karl. Ikonographie der Heiligen. 2 vols. Freiburg im Breisgau, 1926-28.

La Fons, Quentin de. Extraits originaux d'un manuscrit de Quentin de La Fons, intitulé "Histoire particulière de l'église de Saint-Quentin", edited by Ch. Gomart. 2 vols. Saint-Quentin, 1854-56.

Langlois, Charles V. La vie en France au moyen âge, de la fin du xiie au milieu du xive siècle. 4 vols. Paris, 1924-28.

Lantern of Lizt. Edited by Lillian M. Swinburn. London, 1917. Early English Text Society Publications, Vol. CLI.

Latimer, Hugh. Sermons. Edited for the Parker Society by George E. Corrie. 2 vols. Cambridge, 1844-45.

Lay Folks Mass Book. Edited by T. F. Simmons. London, 1879. Early English Text Society Publications, Vol. CXVIII.

Lecoy de la Marche, Albert. La chaire française au moyen âge. 2nd edition. Paris, 1886.

The Ledger-book of Vale Royal Abbey. Edited by John Brownbill. Liverpool, 1914.

Leet Jurisdiction in the City of Norwich during the XIIIth and XIVth Centuries. Edited by William Hudson. London, 1892. Selden Society Publications, Vol. V.

Letters and Papers, Foreign and Domestic, of the Reign of Henry the Eighth. Arranged and catalogued by J. S. Brewer, James Gairdner, and R. H. Brodie. 21 vols. London, 1862-1910.

Lindsay, Thomas M. A History of the Reformation. 2 vols. New York, 1906-1910.

The Little Red Book of Bristol. Edited by Francis B. Bickley. 2 vols. London, 1900.

Lupton, Joseph, H. A Life of John Colet. London, 1887.

Luther, Martin. Werke. 67 vols. Weimar, 1883-1932.

Luther's Primary Works, together with his shorter and larger Catechisms. Translated by Henry Wace and C. Buchheim. London, 1896.

Lutius, Horatius. "De privilegiis scholarium", Tractatus illustrium in utraque tum pontificii, tum caesarei iuris facultate iurisconsultorum, Vol. XVIII, folios 67 v to 90 v.

Lyndwood, William. Provinciale. (Edition with glosses). Oxford, 1679.

——, The text of the canons therein contained, reprinted from the translation made in 1534. Edited by J. V. Bullard and H. C. Bell. London, 1929.

Lyte, H. C. Maxwell. A History of Eton College, 1440-1884. London and New York, 1889.

Magoun, Francis P. "Football in Medieval England and in Middle-English Literature", American Historical Review, Vol. XXXV (1929), pp. 33-45.

Maitland, Frederic W. Domesday Book and Beyond. Cambridge, 1907.

Maitland, Samuel R. Facts and Documents Illustrative of the History, Doctrine, and Rites of the Ancient Albigenses and Waldenses. London, 1832.

Mallet, Charles E. A History of the University of Oxford. 3 vols. London, 1924-27.

Manning, Bernard L. The People's Faith in the Time of Wyclif. Cambridge,
     1919.
Mannyng, Robert, of Brunne. Handlyng Synne. Edited by F. J. Furnivall.
     London, 1901. Early English Text Society Publications, Vols. CXIX,
     CXXIII.
Manuale scholarium. Translated by R. F. Seybolt. Cambridge, 1921.
Marsiglio of Padua. Defensor pacis. Edited by C. W. Previté-Orton. Cam-
     bridge, 1928.
Martin Saint-Léon, Étienne. Histoire des corporations de métiers depuis
     leurs origines jusqu'à leur suppression en 1791 . . . Revised edition.
     Paris, 1922.
Matthew Paris. Chronica majora. Edited by Henry R. Luard. 7 vols.
     London, 1872-83.
Mazzolini, Silvestro da Prierio. Summa summarum que Silvestrina nun-
     cupatur. 2 vols. Lyons, 1528.
Medieval Archives of the University of Oxford. Edited by H. E. Salter.
     2 vols. Oxford, 1920-21. Oxford Historical Society Publications, Vols.
     LXX, LXXIII.
Merton Muniments. Selected and edited for the College by P. S. Allen . . .
     and H. W. Garrod . . . Oxford, 1928. Oxford Historical Society Publi-
     cations, Vol. LXXXVI.
Meyer, Arnold O. Studien zur Vorgeschichte der Reformation. Aus
     schlesischen Quellen. Munich and Berlin, 1903.
Mirk, John. Festial: a Collection of Homilies. Edited by T. Erbe. Lon-
     don, 1905. Early English Text Society Publications, Vol. XCVI.
——, Instructions for Parish Priests. Edited by E. Peacock. London, 1868.
     Early English Text Society Publications, Vol. XXXI.
Missale ad usum insignis ecclesiae Eboracensis. Edited by William G.
     Henderson. 2 vols. Durham, 1874. Surtees Society Publications, Vols.
     LIX-LX.
Monaldus. Summa perutilis atque aurea venerabilis viri fratris Monaldi
     in utroque jure tam civilique canonico. Lyons, 1516?
More, Thomas. English Works. Edited with a modern version of the same
     by W. E. Campbell . . . 2 vols. London, 1927-31.
Mosellanus, Petrus. Paedologia. See R. F. Seyboldt's Renaissance Student
     Life.
Mullinger, James B. The University of Cambridge from the Earliest Times
     to the Royal Injunctions for 1535. 3 vols. Cambridge, 1873.
Munimenta academica: or Documents Illustrative of Academical Life and
     Studies at Oxford. Edited by H. Anstey. 2 vols. London, 1868. Rolls
     Series, Vol. L.
Munimenta gildhallae Londoniensis: Liber albus, Liber custumarum, et Liber
     Horn. Edited by H. T. Riley. 3 vols. London, 1859-1862. Rolls Series,
     Vol. XII.
Napier, Arthur S., ed. "An Old English Homily on the Observance of Sun-
     day", *An English Miscellany, presented to Dr. Furnivall in honor of his
     seventy-fifth birthday*. Oxford, 1901. Pp. 355-362.

Neilson, Nellie. Economic Conditions on the Manors of Ramsey Abbey. Philadelphia, 1898.

Ney, J. "Analekten zur Geschichte des Reichstags zu Speier im Jahre 1526", *Zeitschrift für Kirchengeschichte,* Vol. VIII, pp. 300-317; IX, 137-181.

Northumberland and Durham Deeds. Edited by A. M. Oliver. Newcastle upon Tyne, 1929.

Ogle, Arthur. The Canon Law in Medieval England. An examination of William Lyndwood's "Provinciale", in reply to the late Professor F. W. Maitland. London, 1912.

Old English Homilies and Homiletic Treatises . . . of the Twelfth and Thirteenth Centuries. Translated and edited by R. Morris. London, 1868. Early English Text Society Publications, Vols. XXIX, XXXIV.

Oldradus de Ponte. Consilia, seu responsa, et quaestiones aureae, in quibus ea quae ad quotidianum usum in forensibus negotiis, et controversiis spectant, subtilissime et exactissime perstringuntur. Venice, 1571.

Ordonnances des rois de France de la troisième race, 1051-1514. 21 vols. Paris, 1723-1849.

Owst, Gerald T. Literature and Pulpit in Medieval England. Cambridge, 1933.

——, Preaching in Medieval England. An introduction to sermon manuscripts of the period, ca. 1350-1450. Cambridge, 1926.

Oxford City Documents, Financial and Judicial, 1268-1665. Selected and edited by J. E. Thorold Rogers. Oxford, 1891. Oxford Historical Society Publications, Vol. XVIII.

Palmer, R. Liddesdale. English Monasteries in the Middle Ages. London, 1930.

Patrologiae cursus completus. Series latina. Edited by J. P. Migne. 221 vols. Paris, 1844-64.

Peckham, John. Registrum epistolarum. Edited by C. T. Martin. 3 vols. London, 1882-85. Rolls Series, Vol. LXXVII.

Pelagius, Alvarus. De planctu ecclesiae. 2 vols. Ulm, 1474.

Perdrizet, Paul. Le calendrier de la nation d'Allemagne de l'ancienne Université de Paris. Paris, 1937.

——, Le calendrier parisien à la fin du moyen âge d'après le bréviaire et les livres d'heures. Paris, 1933.

Petrus de Palude. Sermones thesauri novi de tempore, de sanctis, et quadragesimales. Nuremberg, 1496.

Pfülf, Otto. "Die Verehrung des heiligen Joseph in der Geschichte", *Stimmen aus Maria-Laach,* Vol. XXXVIII (1890), pp. 137-161 and 282-302.

Plinius Secundus, C. *Historiae naturalis libri XXXVII.* With the commentary of Jean Hardouin. 10 vols. Paris, 1827-32.

Post, Gaines. "Masters' Salaries and Student-fees in the Medieval Universities," *Speculum,* VII (1932), 181-198.

Potho, presbyter Prumiens. "De statu domus Dei", *Maxima bibliotheca veterum patrum et antiquorum scriptorum ecclesiasticorum.* Lyons, 1677, Vol. XXI, pp. 489-513.

Prantl, Carl. Geschichte der Ludwig-Maximilians-Universität in Ingolstadt, Landshut, München zur Festfeier ihres vierhundertjährigen Bestehens. 2 vols. Munich, 1872.

Priebatsch, Felix. "Staat und Kirche in der Mark Brandenburg am Ende des Mittelalters". *Zeitschrift für Kirchengeschichte*, Vol. XIX (1899), pp. 397-430; XX (1900), 159-185, 329-365; XXI (1901), 43-90.

Rashdall, Hastings. The Universities of Europe in the Middle Ages. A new edition, by F. M. Powicke and A. B. Emden. 3 vols. Oxford, 1936.

Rashdall, Hastings and Rait, Robert S. New College. London, 1901.

Raymond of Pennafort. Summa. Verona, 1744. Tit. XII. "De feriis, et festis, et diebus jejuniorum."

Reber, Balthasar. Felix Hemmerlin von Zürich, Zurich, 1846.

Rebuffi, Pierre. "De privilegiis scholarium", *Tractatus illustrium in utraque tum pontificii, tum caesarei iuris facultate iurisconsultorum*. Vol. XVIII, folios 32v to 67r.

Records of the Borough of Northampton. Vol. I edited by Christopher A. Markham, etc., and Vol. II by J. C. Cox. London and Northampton, 1898.

Records of the City of Norwich. Compiled and edited by W. Hudson and J. C. Tingley. 2 vols. Norwich, 1906-1910.

Recueil de textes relatifs à l'histoire de l'architecture et à la condition des architectes en France, au moyen âge, XIIe-XIIIe siècles. Edited by V. Mortet et P. Deschamps. Paris, 1929.

Regesta Stolbergica: Quellensammlung zur Geschichte der Grafen zu Stolberg im Mittelalter. Prepared and arranged by Botho, Count of Stolberg, Wernigerode und Mülverstedt. Magdeburg, 1885.

Registrum annalium collegii Mertonensis, 1483-1521. Edited by H. E. Salter. Oxford, 1923. Oxford Historical Society Publications, Vol. LXXVI.

Registrum cancellarii Oxoniensis, 1434-1469. Edited by H. E. Salter. 2 vols. Oxford, 1932. Oxford Historical Society Publications, Vols. XCIII, XCIV.

Registrum collegii Exoniensis. Edited by C. W. Boase. New edition. Oxford, 1894. Oxford Historical Society Publications, Vol. XXVII.

Reinerius Sacchoni, "Contra Waldenses haereticos". Edited by J. Gretzer. *Maxima bibliotheca veterum patrum et antiquorum scriptorum ecclesiasticorum*. Vol. XXV (Lyons, 1677), pp. 262-277. (The attribution to Reinerius is incorrect. See W. Preger, "Beiträge zur Geschichte der Waldesier im Mittelalter", *Abhandlungen der königlich-bayerischen Akademie der Wissenschaften*, Hist. Klasse XIII, I (Munich, 1875), 184-250.

Revue de l'art chrétien. Paris, 1857 ff.

Rigaud, Eudes. Regestrum visitationum archiepiscopi Rothomagensis, 1248-1269. Edited by T. Bonnin. Rouen, 1852.

Riley, Henry T. Memorials of London and London Life in the XIIIth, XIVth, and XVth centuries. London, 1868.

Rock, Daniel. The Church of Our Fathers, as seen in St. Osmund's Rite for the Cathedral of Salisbury. 4 vols. New edition. London, 1905.

Rodocanachi, Emmanuel. Les corporations ouvrières à Rome depuis la chute de l'empire romain. 2 vols. Paris, 1894.

Roger of Hoveden. Chronica. Edited by William Stubbs. 4 vols. London, 1868-71.

Roger of Wendover. Liber qui dicitur Flores Historiarum ab anno domini MCLIV. Edited by H. G. Hewlett. 3 vols. London, 1886-89.

Rogers, James E. Thorold. Six Centuries of Work and Wages; A History of English Labour. New York, 1884.

——, A History of Agriculture and Prices in England, 1259-1793. 7 vols. Oxford, 1866-1902.

Le roman de la rose, by Guillaume de Lorris and Jean de Meun. Edited by E. Langlois. 5 vols. Paris, 1914-24. For an English translation, see that by F. S. Ellis. 3 vols. London, 1900.

Sacrist Rolls of Ely. Edited by F. R. Chapman. 2 vols. Cambridge, 1907.

Sacrorum conciliorum nova et amplissima collectio. Edited by J. D. Mansi and others. 31 vols. Florence and Venice, 1759-1798.

Sägmüller, Johannes B. Lehrbuch des katholischen Kirchenrechts. 2 vols. 3rd edition. Freiburg, 1914.

Saint German, Christopher. A Treatyse Concerninge the Power of the Clergye and the Lawes of the Realme. London, 1535.

Salter, Herbert E. Medieval Oxford. Oxford, 1936. Oxford Historical Society Publications, Vol. C.

——, "An Oxford Hall in 1424", *Essays in History,* by R. L. Poole. Edited by H. W. C. Davis. Oxford, 1927. pp. 421-435.

Salzmann, Louis F. English Industries of the Middle Ages. Boston and New York, 1913.

——, English Trade in the Middle Ages. Oxford, 1931.

Sarti, Maurus, and Fattorini, Maurus. De claris archigymnasii Bononiensis professoribus a saeculo XI usque ad saeculum XIV. 2 vols. Bologna, 1888-96.

The Sarum Missal in English, newly translated by Frederick E. Warren. 2 vols. London, 1911.

Savigny, Friedrich K. von. Geschichte des römischen Rechts im Mittelalter. 6 vols. Heidelberg, 1815-31.

Scheible, Johann. Das Kloster, weltlich und geistlich. 12 vols. Stuttgart, 1845.

Schmidt, Charles. Histoire et doctrine de la secte des Cathares ou Albigeois. 2 vols. Paris, 1849.

Schulte, Johann F. von. Die Geschichte der Quellen und Literatur des canonischen Rechts von Gratian bis auf die Gegenwart. 3 vols. Stuttgart, 1875-80.

Scott, G. G. Gleanings from Westminster Abbey. Oxford and London, 1861. (Appendix II, with explanation by Professor Willis).

Select Pleas in Manorial and Other Seignorial Courts. Edited by F. W. Maitland. London, 1889. Selden Society Publications, Vol. II.

Select Pleas of the Crown, A. D. 1200-1225. Edited by F. W. Maitland. London, 1888. Selden Society Publications, Vol. I.

Sermones dominicales dormi secure. (n. p., before 1500). Attributed to John of Verdun (fl. ca. 1330?).

Seybolt, R. F. Renaissance Student Life: A Translation of the *Paedologia* of Petrus Mosellanus. Urbana, 1927.

Shapiro, Jacob S. Social Reform and the Reformation. [n. p.], 1909.

Simons, T. W. Working Days, Holidays, and Vacations in England in the Fourteenth and Fifteenth Centuries. *University of Colorado Studies*, Vol. XXIV (1936), pp. 65-66. (Abstract of an unpublished dissertation.)

Smith, John T. Antiquities of Westminster. London, 1807.

Smith, Joshua Toulmin. English gilds. London, 1870. Early English Text Society Publications, Vol. XL.

——, The Parish. London, 1857.

South, John F. Memorials of the Craft of Surgery in England. London, 1886.

Staley, Edgcombe. The Guilds of Florence. London, 1906.

Statuta antiqua universitatis Oxoniensis. Edited with an introduction by Strickland Gibson. Oxford, 1931.

" Statutes of Exeter College ". *The Register of Walter de Stapeldon, Bishop of Exeter (1307-1326)*. Edited by F. C. Hingeston-Randolph. London, 1892. pp. 303-310.

Statutes of Lincoln Cathedral. Arranged and edited by Henry Bradshaw and Christopher Wordsworth. 3 vols. Cambridge, 1897.

Statutes of the Colleges of Oxford. 3 vols. Oxford, 1853.

Statutes of the Realm [of Great Britain], 1235-1713. Edited by G. Luders, T. E. Tomlins, and others. 11 vols. London, 1810-28.

Statuti dei mercanti di Roma. Edited by G. Gatti. Rome, 1885.

Statuti della Repubblica Fiorentina. Edited by R. Caggese. 2 vols. Florence, 1910-21.

Statuti dell' arte dei medici e speziali. Edited by Raffaele Ciasca. Florence, 1925.

Statuti delle università e dei collegi dello studio bolognese. Edited by C. Malagolo. Bologna, 1888.

Statuti di Bellano e Mandello. Edited by E. Anderloni and V. Adami. Milan, 1932.

Stolle, Konrad. " Chronik ". Edited by L. F. Hesse. *Bibliothek des literarischen Vereins im Stuttgart*. Vol. XXXII, Stuttgart, 1854.

Stow, John. A Survey of London. Edited by W. J. Thoms, London, 1842.

Strutt, Joseph. Sports and Pastimes of the People of England. London, 1845.

Suger, l'Abbé. Oeuvres complètes. Edited by A. Lecoy de la Marche, Paris, 1867.

Summa rudium. Reutlingen, 1487.

Sylvius, Aeneas. Opera omnia. Basil, 1571.

Tauler, Johannes. Predigten. Edited by W. Lehmann. 2 vols. Jena, 1923.

Thomas à Kempis. Opera omnia. Edited by Michael J. Pohl. 7 vols. Freiburg im Breisgau, 1902-22.

Thomas Aquinas. Opera omnia. Edited by S. E. Fretté and Pauli Maré. 34 vols. Paris, 1871-80.

Thorndike, Lynn. Franciscus Florentinus or Paduanus: An Inquisitor of the Fifteenth Century and his Treatise on Astrology and Divination, Magic and Popular Superstition, *Mélanges Mandonnet,* Vol. II (Paris, 1930), pp. 353-369.

Thorne, William. Chronicle of Saint Augustine's Abbey, Canterbury, now rendered into English by A. H. Davis. Oxford, 1934.

Three Early Assize Rolls for the County of Northumberland, Saec. XIII. Edited by William Page. Durham, 1891. Surtees Society Publications, Vol. LXXXVIII.

Thurston, Herbert. "The Medieval Sunday", *The Nineteenth Century,* Vol. XLVI (1899), 36-50.

Tickner, F. W. Social and Industrial History of England. New York, 1923.

Toynbee, Margaret R. S. Louis of Toulouse and the Process of Canonization in the Fourteenth Century. Manchester, 1929.

Vergilius, Polydorus. De rerum inventoribus. Cologne, 1626.

Vergilius Maro, Publius. "Georgica", Loeb edition of *Virgil,* Vol. I (London, 1920), pp. 79-237.

The Vision of William concerning Piers the Plowman. Edited by W. W. Skeat. 3 vols. Oxford, 1886.

Visitation Articles and Injunctions of the Period of the Reformation (1536-1575). Edited by W. H. Frere and W. M. Kennedy. 3 vols. London, 1910. Alcuin Club Collections, Vols. XIV-XVI.

Visitations and Memorials of Southwell Minster. Edited by Arthur F. Leach. London, 1891. Camden Society Publications, Vol. XLVIII.

Walsingham, Thomas. Gesta abbatum monasterii Sancti Albani. Edited by H. T. Riley, 3 vols. London, 1867-1869. Rolls Series, Vol. XXVIII.

——, Historia anglicana, 1272-1422. Edited by H. T. Riley. 2 vols. London, 1863-64. Rolls Series, Vol. XXVIII.

Walter of Henley's Husbandry, together with an anonymous Husbandry, Seneschaucie, and Robert Grosseteste's Rules. With a translation. Edited by E. Lamond, with an introduction by W. Cunningham. London, 1890.

Webster, Hutton. Rest Days: A Study in Early Law and Morality. New York, 1916.

Welter, J. Th. L'Exemplum dans la littérature religieuse et didactique du moyen âge. Paris, 1927.

Willard, James F. The Observance of Holidays and Vacations by the Lower Exchequer, 1327-1336. *University of Colorado Studies,* XXII (1935), pp. 281-87.

William of Wadington. Le manuel des pechiez. Printed with Robert Mannyng of Brunne's *Handlyng Synne.*

William of Wykeham. Register, Edited by T. F. Kirby. 2 vols. London, 1896-99. Hampshire Record Society Publications, Vols. XI and XIII.

Winkelmann, Eduard. Urkundenbuch der Universität Heidelberg. 2 vols. Heidelberg, 1886.

Wood, Anthony. The History and Antiquities of the University of Oxford. Edited by John Gutch. 2 vols. Oxford, 1792-96.

Wordsworth, Christopher, and Littlehales, Henry. Old Servicebooks of the English Church. London, 1904.

Wright, Thomas. Political Poems and Songs Relating to English History, composed during the period from the accession of Edward III to that of Richard III. Edited by Thomas Wright. 2 vols. London, 1859-61. Rolls Series, Vol. XIV.

——, A Selection of Latin Stories, from Manuscripts of the Thirteenth and Fourteenth Centuries. London, 1842.

Wyclif, John. The English Works Hitherto Unprinted. Edited by F. D. Matthew. London, 1880. Early English Text Society Publications, Vol. LXXIV.

——, Select English Works. Edited by Thomas Arnold. 3 vols. Oxford, 1869.

Wylie, James H. History of England under Henry IV. 4 vols. London, 1884-98.

Young, Karl. The Drama of the Medieval Church. 2 vols. Oxford, 1933.

Zabarella, Francesco. "Capita agendorum in concilio generali Constantiensi de reformatione ecclesiae", H. von der Hardt, *Magnum oecumenicum Constantiense consilium de universali ecclesiae reformatione, unione, et fide*, Vol. I, cols. 490-536.

Zarncke, Friedrich. Die deutschen Universitäten im Mittelalter. Leipzig, 1857.

——, ed. Die Statutenbücher der Universität Leipzig aus den ersten 150 Jahren ihres Bestehens . . . Leipzig, 1861.

Zedler, Johann Heinrich. Grosses vollständiges Universal-Lexicon aller Wissenschafften und Künste. 64 vols. Halle und Leipzig, 1732-50.

Zeitschrift für Kirchengeschichte. Edited by T. Brieger, B. Bess, and L. Zscharnack et al. 57 vols. Gotha, 1877 ff.

INDEX

A

Abram, A., 70 *n*
Abrogation, *see* Holiday reduction
Addy, S. O., 98 *n*
Aeneas Sylvius, 105 *n*
Agatha's Day, St., 87
Agincourt, battle of, 85 *n*
Agricultural work, 14 *n*, 33, 75, 102;
and multiplicity of holidays, 92 ff.;
see also Harvest; Peasants
Agrippa of Nettesheim, 120
Ailly, Pierre d', 16; vs. new holidays,
83; on canonization, 107; at Council of Constance, 108
Alban, St., 11
Albert of Saxony, 58 *n*, 59
Albertus Magnus, " Sermons," 21 *n*
Albigensians, 29 *n*, 87 *n*, 105 *n*
Albrecht of Prussia, 113
Alexander III, 40
Alexander of Hales, 17, 29*n*, 33*n*,
36 *n*, 41 *n*, 42 *n*
All Soul's College, Oxford, 51 *n*
Alvarus Pelagius, *see* Pelayo, Alvaro
Amaury of Bène, 58
Andrea, Giovanni d', 23, 11 *n*
Angelo Carletti di Chivasso, 31*n*, 36*n*,
37 *n*, 38, 39, 40 *n*, 42 *n*, 43 *n*, 53 *n*,
56 *n*; on markets, 78 f., 79 *n*
Angers, Univ. of, church attendance,
54 *n*; lectures, 61
Animals, holiday work of, 34, 38;
Cato on, 94 *n*
Annunciation, Feast of, 32
Anselm, 10 *n*
Anthony of Padua, St., 12, 87
Antonino of Florence, 13, 18, 24;
Confessionale, 18 *n*, 31 *n*; *Summa*,
33 *n*, 35 *n*; 40 *n*, 41 *n*, 44 *n*, 47 *n*,
73 *n*; on holiday travel, 43; on
games, 46; on lecture fees, 56;
on neglect of holidays, 66 *n*; on
abuse of holidays, 75
Apelles, 62
Apostles, the, 10, 105, 117
Apostolic See, 11
Apothecaries, 41
Aquinas, Thomas, 12, 23, 29 *n*, 39 *n*;
on care of the sick, 41; canonization of, 103 *n*
Archdeacon's court, *see* Court
Archery, 46, 111
Aristotle, 58, 61

B

Artisans, 33, 73, 112; complaints
about number of holidays, 93 f.
Arundel, Thomas, 67, 74
Ascension Day, 29; markets on, 79;
Waldensians and, 105
Assizes, on Sunday, 99
Assumption, Feast of, 79, 115
Astesano d' Asti, 11 *n*, 34 *n*, 35 f.,
43 *n*.
Astrology, 60 f.
Astronomy, 59
Auctarium chart. univ. Paris., 15 *n*,
57 *n*, 58 *n*
Audelay, John, 28 *n*
Augustine, St., on servile work, 34;
on dancing and dramatic performances, 49
Avicenna, 60
Avignon, 19; wages at, 97 *n*
Avignon, Council of, 90
Azo of Bologna, 44 *n*

Bailey, N., 26 *n*
Bakers, 70, 75, 76, 112
Baldo degli Ubaldi, 18
Ball, John, 72
Ball game, 68
Balliol College, Oxford, 54 *n*
Bankers, 41
Baptista de Salis, 24 *n*, 37 *n*, 38 *n*,
39 *n*, 43 *n*, 47 *n*, 52 *n*, 55 *n*, 56 *n*, 109
Barbara, St., 110
Barbers, 73, 73 *n*, 74 f.
Barclay, Alexander, 27, 66 *n*, 68 *n*,
69 *n*
Baring-Gould, S., 13 *n*
Bartholomew, St., Feast of, 115
Bartolo da Sassoferrato, 17, 18 *n*,
44 *n*
Bartolomeo of Brescia, 61
Bartolomeo Pisano, 36 *n*, 37 *n*, 38 *n*,
39, 39 *n*, 43 *n*, 55 *n*, 102; on holiday
sin, 35 *n*; on sports, 46
Basel, Council of, 20, 113; on Feast
of Fools, 91; and holiday reduction, 109
Bax, E. B., 71 *n*, 95 *n*
Becket, Thomas à, *see* Thomas à
Becket
Bellano, statutes of, 44 *n*
Benedict XIII, 19
Benedict, St., 34
Bennett, H. S., 14 *n*, 95 *n*